Creating a Learning-Centered Classroom

Creating a Learning-Centered Classroom:

A PRACTICAL GUIDE FOR TEACHERS

HOWARD E. BLAKE

A HART BOOK

A & W VISUAL LIBRARY • NEW YORK

To Betty, Muba, Chip, and Genie

PUBLISHED BY
A & W PUBLISHERS, INC.
95 MADISON AVENUE
NEW YORK, NEW YORK 10016

LIBRARY OF CONGRESS CATALOG CARD NUMBER: 76-6698
ISBN: 0-89104-179-6

PRINTED IN THE UNITED STATES OF AMERICA

CONTENTS

PREFACE

Explaining learning centers is like describing an elephant to someone who's never seen one. If you've already seen the elephant, hopefully you'll find this book will help to reinforce what you're doing, and perhaps will add a number of ideas to your own that will help you do a better job.

If you've never seen the elephant, that is, if you've done little or no learning center teaching, this book will tell you what you need to know, and show you how easy it is to make the transition and move in a step-by-step fashion from a quite simple model to a more sophisticated one.

Whether you are an elementary, middle school, or a secondary teacher, whether you are a pre-service or in-service teacher, whether you teach in a traditional or an open space classroom, whether you are a teacher or a principal, you should find appropriate ideas in this book that will help you build a better learning environment.

Having been a teacher and a principal in elementary, junior, and senior high schools, and having conducted hundreds of in-service workshops and graduate courses on learning centers, I have developed the firm belief that seldom do two teachers teach alike. The individual differences among teachers are as significant as those among children. Consequently, this book takes the view that there is more than one model for the learning centered classroom, and that teachers should have the freedom to create their own models, commensurate with their own knowledge, experience, teaching styles, and with the needs of their children. Further, this book makes the plea that schools be continuously changing institutions. But change cannot be mandated. It has to be a democratic process involving all school personnel. Change occurs gradually and requires adequate preparation.

It is also the viewpoint of this author that [individualized instruction is the best method for meeting the needs of children, and that learning centers offer the teacher an effective and easy method for individualizing.

The writing of this book is the direct outcome of having worked with many exciting and stimulating teachers in workshops and in classrooms. Every one of them has contributed in some way to this book. Their questions and constant search for improved methods have been a source of inspiration for me and I am deeply indebted to every one of them.

I especially wish to thank Dan Condon, Sharon Guarante, Jim MacCall, Beth McFarland, Marianne Straub, Betty Van Arsdale, and Joan Verna for their able and unselfish assistance with the sample learning centers in the book. Their understanding of the learning center process is highly reflected in the quality of the centers. I respect them for their brilliance as learning center teachers as well as for their friendship.

I would like to express my deepest appreciation to my wife, Betty, and to our two children, Chip and Genie, for the encouragement and assistance they give me every day. Without them, my inspiration might have faltered.

H.E.B

NOTE

Throughout this book, the anonymous teacher or student has been referred to as "he." This is not to slight females in any way. The decision was reluctantly made in the absence of a feasible means for resolving the problem of the indefinite pronoun. Care has been taken to avoid stereotyping, and it is hoped that this book makes its contribution in promoting all humanistic goals in education.

I

The Learning Centered Classroom—
What Is It?

Recently, I conducted a one-month workshop on learning centers, and I asked the participants, who were for the most part experienced teachers, to write a definition of the learning-centered classroom. Here are some of the answers:

A place where learning comes alive—a place to learn!

A place where children learn a great deal without being aware of it. They learn to learn.

A classroom in which activities are provided to supplement teacher instruction. Through these activities the children learn to follow directions, develop self-confidence and express their individuality. Even though there is more movement by the children, it is more structured than the conventional classroom.

A classroom in which the children are motivated to learn independently by going from one area to another. Each area has been set up attractively in such a way as to enable children to learn by self-discovery. There is immediate feedback of success or failure through a self-check system. There must be some structure to keep the flow of children even and to keep a record of where they are, have been, and what they need to do.

It is a classroom where independent activities and centers

are constructed according to the needs of the children. During a designated time each day, or during free time, each child works on a number of centers according to his contract. Each child checks his own work when completed, and then places it in a designated place for further diagnosis by the teacher.

It it is one way of learning; but it cannot be used alone; direct teaching is also needed. It needs much supervision. It is a way of reinforcement of learning in that children work independently on activities that coincide with what they have been or are being taught. It is a way of teaching a skill or concept without the teacher always standing in front of the room.

It is one in which the children are given a choice in what they can'do. The teacher is a resource person, not a lecturer. Materials are available for children to work with creatively, and children are allowed the freedom, within limits, to move around in the classroom.

It is one which creates and instills a feeling of responsibility and promotes individualized instruction. A skilled observer walking into this classroom would immediately have the feeling that learning was taking place.

No two of these statements are the same, yet they all reflect common points of view about how teaching and learning occur in classrooms which contain learning centers. These definitions also reveal that there are wide differences among teachers about the essence of the learning centered classroom. Each teacher emphasizes the things he considers to be of importance.

The point of view in this book is that this is just as it should be. No single definition will suffice. There are many different kinds of learning centers, and there are many different ways of setting up learning centers. Each teacher can create the kind of classroom environment that suits his own and his students' interests and learning styles. The important thing is that the teacher have a clear understanding of what he is doing and why. Setting up learning centers is not a mechanical thing that a teacher can do simply by copying something he has observed somewhere. There is an underlying philosophy of education that permeates, inspires and invigorates the learning-centered approach to teaching. Once a teacher grasps and accepts the essence of the approach, he is free to interpret it into concrete action in his classroom according to his own pace and style. Teachers have different tolerances for activity or movement, different outlets for creativity, different talents and interests. Just as the individuality of the child is to be respected and nurtured within social limits, so is the personality of the teacher given expression in the organization of his classroom.

In this chapter, the basic concepts underlying the learning-centered classroom will be explained so that the spirit and not just the letter of the law may be implemented. Then, when in subsequent chapters specific models are presented, the teacher will understand that they are to be used simply as sources of inspiration for his own more appropriate, more timely and, hopefully, more creative endeavors. Terms will be defined and clarified so that the teacher may know not only what a learning-centered classroom is, but also what it is not.

Why Have Learning Centers?

Learning centers allow the classroom to be child-centered rather than teacher-centered. Learning centers are based upon the Piagetian[1] concept that the child should be the chief agent in his own education, and that different children rarely develop or learn in the same way. The role of the teacher is equally important in the traditional classroom and in the learning-centered classroom, but it is vastly different in each. No longer

---

1. Piaget, Jean, *The Language and Thought of the Child*, London, Routledge and Kegan Paul, Ltd., 1959.

does the teacher spend a major part of his time in front of the entire class engaged in the nearly impossible task of "emceeing", as Moffett[1] puts it. No longer does the teacher perceive himself as a relay transmitter between the textbook and the child. In the learning-centered classroom the teacher is a guide and a facilitator, setting up materials and activities that meet the children's perceived needs and interests and that encourage children to explore exciting new areas. As children engage in independent activities the teacher circulates and interacts with them individually or in small groups, watching, commenting, diagnosing, tutoring, asking, making suggestions.

Learning centers help individualize learning. To establish a system that teaches the same things to some 35-odd students at the same time and expects them to learn at the same pace and in the same way is to court frustration and hostility. The child who learns quickly becomes bored, impatient, supercilious, while the slower child feels pressured, anxious, defensive. Learning centers allow children to learn many of the same things, but at their own rate, with as much or as little teacher help as needed. Learning becomes personalized as each child works at his own tasks, pacing himself. Learning becomes more meaningful and challenging as each child competes only with himself. The joy of mastering a skill or completing a project is intrinsic, enriching the child and enhancing his self-esteem. Children begin to understand that learning is something you do to please yourself, not to please or show off to others. A child who works for the sheer joy of self-fulfillment and experiences gratification in his own growing aptitudes will be self-motivated, productive, happy. With children working individually, the teacher is able to divide his time among them more appropriately. The relationship between pupil and teacher becomes warmer, more personal, more trusting.

---

1. Moffett, James, *A Student-Centered Language Arts Curriculum, K-13*, Boston, Houghton Mifflin, 1968, p. 46.

Learning centers help individualize learning. To establish a system that teaches the same things to some 35 odd students at the same time and expects them to learn at the same pace and in the same way is to court frustration and hostility. The child who learns quickly becomes bored, impatient, supercilious, while the slower child feels pressured, anxious, defensive. Learning centers allow children to learn many of the same things, but at their own rate, with as much or as little teacher help as needed. Learning becomes personalized as each child works at his own tasks, pacing himself. Learning becomes more meaningful and challenging as each child competes only with himself. The joy of mastering a skill or completing a project is intrinsic, enriching the child and enhancing his self-esteem. Children begin to understand that learning is something you do to please yourself, not to please or show off to others. A child who works for the sheer joy of self-fulfillment, and experiences gratification in his own growing aptitudes will be self-motivated, productive, happy. With children working individually, the teacher is able to divide his time among them more appropriately. The relationship between pupil and teacher becomes warmer, more personal, more trusting.

Learning centers allow for active participation by children. Children don't learn much by being talked at; they need to explore, to question, to experiment and formulate their own solutions. Good teaching is not telling. All that this requires of children is that they memorize. Children learn better and remember what they have learned longer when they participate actively in the pursuit of knowledge. We all tend to forget what we are told, but we remember what we ourselves have discovered. Research shows that immediately after hearing something, the average listener is only able to remember about 50%, and that this rate drops to about 25% shortly afterwards.[1]

---

1. Nichols, Ralph and Leonard Evans, *Are You Listening?*, New York, McGraw-Hill, 1957, p. 15.

Some educators feel that this drop may occur as quickly as 48 hours after the first hearing.

Furthermore, a child who is posing questions and exploring hypotheses is learning more than information; he is learning how to learn. Children cannot just be listeners. They have to be producers as well as consumers. Learning centers permit teachers to get off center stage and put the child at the center of his learning.

Research has shown that in the typical traditional classroom 70% of the talking is done by teachers. This would leave about 1% for each of the 30 children; but the study showed that only 18 of 34 children actually did the rest of the talking. Thus almost half the class never expressed themselves at all. Further results of this study revealed that for every 100 questions asked, teachers asked 96, with only four coming from the children. Most of the questions asked were factual, with very few being open-ended. This study raised the very pertinent question, "If teachers and textbooks do all the inquiring, exposing, persuading, and evoking, what is left for the child?"[1]

Learning centers encourage independence in learning. Much of the responsibility for learning is put in the hands of the learner. When a child depends constantly on the teacher to tell him what, when and how to do everything, the child does not feel very responsible for his own learning. As children become more experienced in working in learning centers, they are allowed more freedom and more choices. They have opportunities for much needed experiences in decision making, in goal setting, and in planning and organizing their own educational experiences. They learn to cope and to rely less on minute by minute direction from the teacher. In this kind of setup, children no longer view teachers solely as authoritarian figures; greater trust, respect and affection develop between teachers and children.

---

1. Kean, John M., "Schools, Children, and Communication," *Educational Leadership*, April, 1967.

⭐ *Learning centers humanize education.* The American social system is predicated on a profound concern for the rights and integrity of the individual. The job of the school should be to encourage the flowering of each individual child. When a classroom is organized so that children are expected to sit quietly in their seats most of the day, have no choice in what they do or learn, all work on the same things, and, in short, are all poured into the same mold, they become dehumanized, their individualities violated.

Children learn by doing and talking, not by sitting still and listening. Learning centers provide a more flexible learning environment, adaptable to individual differences. They offer a more life-like setup, reducing the dichotomy between home and school. Learning centers make movement legitimate. Growing bodies are restless. Even traditional teachers recognize this and periodically provide physical diversions such as "Simon Says" or "The Dog and the Bone." But these teacher-led activities still require children all to do the same thing at the same time. In a learning-centered classroom children move about, getting materials, finding a good place to work, researching questions, working on projects, chatting with and helping each other, conferring with the teacher. Social and cognitive growth are promoted when the learner can be physically and socially active, and when the sterile formal classroom is reorganized into interesting and esthetically appealing nooks and corners.

⭐ *Learning centers reduce discipline problems.* Teachers have reported to me that after they have introduced learning centers into their classrooms the number of discipline problems has noticeably diminished. There are many reasons for this but they all seem to add up to the fact that learning centers provide a more congenial environment for youngsters. Of course learning centers are no panacea and there will always be certain children with deep-rooted problems that prevent them from responding positively to any learning organization, but centers do seem to make a significant difference in terms of the general school population. When children are free to move about and talk, when they have greater choice in what they can do, when what they can do suits their needs and abilities more precisely, they take a greater interest in their work and are more responsive and responsible. In short, happy, busy children are less likely to get into mischief. Teachers seem to be more relaxed, too, and children cannot fail to respond to the change in the teachers' relationship with them.

Learning centers are more suited to present world conditions. Schools have often been accused of being the means through which society can maintain the status quo. In fact, far from being the vanguard for constructive change, which is some people's concept of the appropriate role of education, schools are often woefully behind the times. The present generation has gone through a social revolution and is living in a more open society, reflected in current fashions in music, clothing, entertainment, art. While interpersonal relations are more informal and regulations more relaxed, the child's world is actually more complex and he has far more difficult decisions to make with far less guidance. Studies indicate that children are reaching physical maturity at younger and younger ages. Their needs in the real world are vastly different today, and schools have to be ready to meet these needs. Closed, authoritarian systems which would have children line up, sit quietly for long periods, work like robots on the same assignment, keep their ideas and opinions to themselves, ill prepare them to function in the open society which exists outside the school walls. Unless schools operate in as open a manner as the society in which children live, many children will not learn what they should in school and will come to regard school as a place where they mark time until they get out into the real world.

In a learning-centered classroom an effort is made to provide activities which evolve from students' actual needs and interests. Students are given many opportunities for making choices and decisions and for playing an active role in their own education. Not only do they master academic skills, but they develop the social and intellectual skills (independence, responsibility, creativity, resourcefulness) that are essential in a democratic society.

Learning centers help improve the quality of education. The teaching profession, like any other profession or business, must seek the means for its own improvement if it is to avoid becoming obsolete. It is a dismaying fact that traditional education which focused on skill building and academic achievement (in contrast to personal enrichment, stressed by progressive movements) failed in too many cases to reach these objectives. A striking example is the reading program. A survey of reading achievement reported by the National Assessment of Educational Progress (NAEP)[1] indicated that 20 to 30% of young people, ages 9, 13, 17, and 26-35, could not satisfactorily complete various reading tasks. This source further reports that a 1970 Harris poll revealed that 19 million adults in the U.S. are functionally illiterate. An international survey showed that the reading achievement of U.S. 10-year olds was below that of their counterparts in nine other countries; U.S. 14-year olds did more poorly than their peers in three other countries; and the achievement of U.S. students at the end of secondary level fell below that of students in twelve other countries.

Although there is not as yet objective evidence to indicate that children's achievement does improve when they have been taught in learning-centered classrooms, the subjective evidence—teacher and pupil enthusiasm—makes it a worthwhile educational experiement. It would certainly seem likely that pupils working at tasks of their own choice at levels specifically designed for them will inevitably do well. Creating a learning-

---

1. "Reading Becomes Top Educational Priority," *NAEP Bulletin*, September, 1973, p. 1.

centered classroom offers the possibility that each child will develop his full potential as a learner (in terms of academic skills) and as a human being (in terms of character development). It is an educational alternative well worth trying.

Essential Elements in a Learning-Centered Approach

Learning center teaching is more an attitude on the part of the teacher than a system of teaching. Creating centers is an approach for dealing with children's needs, not just a way of organizing a classroom. A teacher who holds the traditional ideas about how children learn and about the role of the teacher may set up learning centers but they will be mechanical and sterile and will make no basic change in the climate of learning. Attitude and system must blend together as one. Repackaging old materials in new wrappings is pursuing change without understanding why and what kind of change is needed. Teaching through learning centers is not just a matter of plugging into a new system. The teacher has to hold specific beliefs which he seeks to implement. He has to believe that children should be treated as individuals, and he should want to pay more than lip service to this belief. He should be willing to listen to children, to learn along with them, respect their needs, ideas, feelings. He should believe that the major role of the teacher is not to disseminate information, but to lead children to learn through their own acts of inquiry and discovery. He should feel that in terms of educational goals the cultivation of life-long values, attitudes and character traits is as important as the acquisition of facts and skills, and that the qualities of independent inquiry, responsibility, creativity, and the skills of goal setting, problem solving, decision-making are best promoted when the learner is not a passive receptacle but an active explorer.

The teacher who holds these beliefs and wants to translate them into concrete action in the classroom needs to be extremely resourceful. He needs to be excited by the challenge of bringing both inspiration and sustenance to some 30-odd individuals in his classroom. Planning for each child's needs places much greater demands on a teacher than does following a syllabus or course of study. Allowing children to learn on their own, to move about freely, to participate more actively in planning, requires both faith and skill. To create learning centers that are appropriate as well as challenging, a teacher needs imagination as well as knowledge. The teacher needs to be able to evaluate each pupil's needs and to create materials and activities that will meet current interests and abilities and stimulate new ones. To do this the teacher should have adequate knowledge of available materials, in print and non-print media, and a good eye for identifying "junk" materials from school, home or neighborhood that may be used to enhance learning centers. Most teachers *can* do all this and enjoy the fun and challenge of teaching in this way.

Creating learning centers is not just organizing activities and space; it is developing specific objectives based on pupil assessment. It is a well known premise that if you know what you're after in teaching, you have a better chance of achieving it. Centers are not to be regarded as materials that provide a series of interesting, unrelated tasks for children. They are not a hodge-podge of all the conceivable ideas and activities the teacher might think up. Centers are created to meet specific curriculum objectives after careful pupil evaluation.

Learning centers require a great deal of structure. To the non-trained observer the learning-centered classroom bears a strong resemblance to Grand Central Station, with everyone going hither and yon without any apparent direction, and with no one knowing just what is going on. Actually the comparison is not so farfetched, for beneath the surface chaos of Grand Central Station, there is order; there is a schedule and everyone actually does know exactly where he is going and when.

In the Grand Central Station classroom each child knows exactly what he is supposed to be doing, and the teacher has the overall plan. Children learn the same skills and concepts in a learning-centered program as they do in a traditional program, but they learn them in a different, more meaningful way— through direct participation in activities geared to each individual's actual level. This means that the teacher plans well in advance, uses a greater variety of materials (many home-made), makes maximum use of space (including floor, walls, cabinets, bulletin boards, easels, dividers, doors, shelves, tables, lamps, carpet, pillows, hangings), and has a thorough analysis and record of each child's needs and progress.

Not all teachers and pupils are comfortable in the Grand Central Station atmosphere of the learning-centered classroom. But the fact is that although there are things all learning-centered classrooms have in common, no two are identical. Each teacher patterns his room to suit his own and his pupils' needs. While some classrooms give the appearance of turmoil, others are very orderly, and all should reflect careful organization underlying a stimulating exterior.

Learning centers permit children to work independently at activities tailored to their needs and interests, and to evaluate their own progress. In the traditional classroom where everyone is working on the same thing, there is often a gap between the time the child does something and the time he finds out how well he did it. Learning cannot be very effective or meaningful under these conditions. When children get immediate feedback, greater success and pleasure in learning are assured. In the learning-centered classroom, the teacher circulates and interacts with the children, observing, checking, helping. Of course, the teacher often feels he should have been an octopus.

In addition, whenever possible provision is made for the child to evaluate himself. It is very easy to provide answer keys for some types of learning centers. An ingenious teacher can also figure out ways of equipping even the more complex learning centers with the means for student self-check. Being able to correct one's errors or improve one's efforts while still engaged in the activity is a tremendous aid in learning and also builds self-esteem. Children begin to feel more responsible for their own learning and take great pride in their progress.

Clarification of Terms and Misconceptions

Learning centers mean different things to different people. This is natural, and desirable. However, in order that the reader understand the point of view in this book certain terms will be defined and some concepts clarified.

Learning centers share certain elements of open education, but they are not the same as the British Integrated Day Model. The philosophy underlying the British Integrated Day approach and the philosophy underlying the learning-centered approach are compatible, even overlapping. However, having observed at first-hand the British approach,[1] I believe that learning centers represent a simpler, more feasible move toward educational change. The British approach requires extensive teacher training, whereas the theory and methodology of learning centers are more easily accessible to both experienced and new teachers.

Learning center and activity center are synonymous terms. Different school systems use different terms, sometimes to mean the same thing, sometimes to mean different things. It doesn't matter what nomenclature is used, provided whatever terms are used are clearly understood and agreed upon. While some learning centers involve simple, short-term activities, and other learning center activities are more complex and of longer dura-

1. Blake, Howard E., "Written Compensation in British Primary Schools," *Elementary English*, October, 1971, pp. 605-616.

tion, for the purposes of this book the same term may be applied—learning center or activity center.

Learning center may refer to the activity itself or to the area within the classroom which houses the learning center. For example, arranged on a bulletin board or on a table there might be a "Tall Tales" learning center in which children become involved in reading tall tales and in creating original tales of their own. Or, the classroom may be divided up into areas for social studies, language arts, etc., and within each of these areas are materials and activities for that particular curriculum area.

Sometimes when a teacher first begins to use the learning center method it is easier (for both teacher and pupils) to start with a variety of activities within just one curriculum area. Later on activities in other curricular areas may be added. Often an activity involves skills in many different curricular areas all at the same time and is not easily classifiable as language arts, social studies or math—for example: Find out what city or country the parents of all the children in this class were born in. Locate these places on the map. Make a chart or graph to show the distribution.

This is a classic example of "a rose by any other name would smell as sweet." It doesn't really matter what terms are used, provided the essence is appreciated.

Learning centers may provide independent activities for reinforcing previously taught skills and concepts; or they may introduce new skills and concepts; or they may stimulate new interests and skills. Repetition is very important in learning. It has been estimated that to learn a given skill or concept bright children require eight to ten repetitions, average children 25 to 30 repetitions, and slower children 50 to 60 repetitions.

To meet these differing needs, centers can provide interesting alternatives for repetition which could make the difference between turning a child on to learning or turning him off. By providing a variety of materials and activities involving specific reading skills, map skills, number facts, topics in science such as magnetism and electrical circuits, the children who need it are given additional practice. In this way learning is both more interesting and more effective.

Centers also provide students with the opportunity for in-depth study of subjects. Students who happen to be especially interested in some special subject—Civil War buffs, for example, or sports fans, or space enthusiasts—and students who complete their work quickly, can work on projects designed by themselves or with teacher help.

With the increasing recognition that affective development is as important as intellectual growth, the fostering of the creative arts has come into its own. We recognize that not only do children need to learn how to learn, but also how to lead full, productive lives and use their time in ways that are gratifying. Centers are an excellent means for exposing children to a variety of activities—photography, music, dramatics, creative writing, sewing, etc.—so that they might develop lasting interests, hobbies, talents.

Learning centers do not necessarily occupy the entire school day; direct teaching also takes place. Creating learning centers is a very adaptable teaching tool. Each teacher has the option of designing the particular setup that suits him and his pupils. Some teachers devote a small part of the day to learning centers; others devote the entire day to learning-centered teaching. Generally, in the beginning a short time is allotted to learning center activities. As the teacher gets to know his pupils better and is able to create and assemble more and more materials and activities to meet their specific needs, the time spent in learning-centered teaching increases. Nevertheless, there is always room and need for some direct teaching. There are certain activities that cannot be conducted individually but require group participation, such as dramatizing a story, holding a debate, role-play, etc. The social interaction that comes when children are engaged in an activity together is invaluable. As children listen to each other, ask questions, state opinions, challenge each other and explain their points of view, they are gaining important social and intellectual insights. They are learning the skills of critical evaluation, decision making, problem solving, and they are learning where they stand in relation to each other.

Also, there are certain skills that are best introduced to the group (small or large) as a whole initially. Then they may be reinforced through individualized learning center activities. For example, teaching a new game, or how to write a haiku poem, or tackling common spelling errors, or following directions, are best demonstrated with a group of children. As the children are involved in the activity together, the teacher observes them and can plan for further individual reinforcement in learning centers.

Thus, moving toward a learning-centered approach can be a gradual process, tailor-made to each teacher's specifications. However, what it does require is a basic change in the teacher's attitudes toward teaching and learning. The precepts upon which learning-centered teaching are based should pervade the entire day. It is virtually impossible to conduct successful learning centers if the teacher's attitudes in direct teaching are inconsistent with the learning-centered approach.

Learning centers do not represent a brand new approach to education. There is really nothing difficult or mystifying about adopting a learning-centered approach. The teacher in the one-room schoolhouse with children of all different ages and abilities used this approach very skillfully. Most good teaching which seeks to meet the actual needs of children uses this approach. What the learning-centered approach does is to combine good teaching techniques with certain principles of how children learn, of the role of the teacher, of the use of materials, and of the goals of education. Teachers who are eager to organize their classrooms so as to guarantee each child the kind of quality education that will enable him to reach his full potential as a learner and as a human being will find the learning-centered approach a practical and exciting direction in which to move.

In Conclusion

At this point it might be a good exercise for the reader to try to formulate his own definition of the learning-centered classroom. This chapter has attempted to present the rationale for learning-centered education. Learning centers are not the final word in education. Hopefully the profession, having begun a serious program of self-evaluation and change, will continue to evolve the particular forms that are consonant with prevailing conditions and needs. To the teacher who would like to reshape his classroom to make it one in which children develop better self-concepts, are treated more humanistically, and become better educated persons, the learning-centered approach offers great promise.

It will have been noted that the "whys" of the learning center have been stressed. The remainder of this book will show the "hows" of putting this theory into action. However fervent his beliefs, every teacher needs concrete help in implementing theory into practice. But the teacher who really grasps the fundamental philosophy will eventually find it very easy and exciting to continually produce learning centers of his own creation.

One word of caution—parents should be fully educated in the whys and wherefores of the learning-centered classroom. They have the right to know what kind of education their children are receiving. When they understand the purpose and the method, they can be of invaluable aid in giving both moral support and volunteer help in the program.

II

Before You Start

Assuming that you are convinced that learning-centered teaching is for you, where and how do you begin?

Gradual Progression

An important rule is: *Start gradually*. Don't try to convert your room to learning centers in two weeks. Hopefully, you will not be instructed by your administrator to start your learning centers "by next Tuesday," or even "by next September." It takes time and training. But be willing to try, to be wrong, and to change or refine your plan as you gain experience. Spend time learning about this approach and gathering and making materials. Don't start your learning centers until you feel ready and confident in your abilities.

Class Assessment

Before you can know which learning centers to create you have to know what your class needs. *Assessment of the class* is a very critical part of the plan and needs much time. Some persons feel that intuition is enough. Intuition is one means of assessment. When coupled with other more objective assessment techniques, it can be an invaluable means for deciding what to teach.

Assessment identifies the needs of the class, suggests which centers to set up and what to include in them, and indicates which groups might work well together for direct instruction or independent learning. Without careful and adequate assessment, learning centers can become a hodgepodge of this and that idea or activity and the program may lack focus or direction.

Assessment helps get away from the lock-step of grade levels by recognizing that children progress at different rates, enabling the teacher to meet children where they actually are regardless of chronological age. It gives the teacher the security of knowing that the centers he makes are appropriate. Centers that are beyond or below the children's level can dampen enthusiasm.

Two kinds of assessment can be used: formal and informal. Formal testing includes the use of standardized tests. It is not usually necessary to give these tests just for setting up centers, for most schools have an annual testing program and results are available either in cumulative records or on computer print-out sheets. The usefulness of these measurements is questionable, especially since they serve mostly to compare children's performance on certain circumscribed tasks to a so-called norm, whereas we are interested in the individual child's needs. However, used judiciously they may help to indicate children's rates of progress and areas of strength or weakness.

Informal tests that are more flexible and that can be given more frequently are more useful. Among such tests are informal reading inventories,[1] phonics inventories,[2] word recognition tests.[3] Teacher-made tests, criterion-referenced tests measuring

1. For example, see Johnson, Marjorie S. and Roy A. Kress, *Informal Reading Inventories*, Newark, Del. International Reading Association, 1965.

2. For example, see *Botel Phonics Inventory*, Chicago, Follett Publishing Co., 1966 and *McCullough Word Analysis Tests*, Princeton, N.J., Personnel Press, Inc., 1963.

3. For example, see *Dolch List of 220 Basic Words*, Champaign, Ill. and the Kucera-Francis Word List in P.D. Johnson, "The Dolch List Reexamined," *Reading Teacher*, February 1971, pp. 449-457.

mastery of specific skills such as recognition of main idea in a paragraph, or identification of compound words, and tests used upon completion of a basic text are very valuable.

Perhaps the most important and reliable assessment tool is teacher observation and judgment, when the teacher is experienced and knowledgeable enough to know what to look for.

Developing a Check-List

You may remember (and sympathize with) the octopus who could never walk again after he was asked how he knew which foot to use first. Every activity—physical, intellectual, social—can be broken down in terms of its component skills, which often follow a specific sequence of development. Yet, like the octopus, if we had to stop to think about each skill and consciously analyze it, we might suffer a loss of spontaneity and efficiency in performance. That is, as long as things were going along all right. When something is wrong, or progress just isn't what it should be, the specific area of difficulty has to be identified. Then to restore or achieve the desired level of functioning, it may be necessary to isolate and do something to strengthen the weakened component skill.

One of the hallmarks of an experienced teacher is the ability to recognize and know how to use part-whole relationships, to integrate skill building with activity teaching. Generally, new teachers tend to focus on one or the other, either initiating activities with little awareness of the level of skills required, or using isolated skill building exercises and losing the forest for the trees. It is very important that the teacher be able to observe an activity and mentally note the specific component skills involved. It is important that the teacher know both how to promote specific skills within broad activities, and when and how to isolate a skill for drill.

The teacher should become familiar with the sequence of skills in each subject matter area. This is not so hard to do; the information is available in many sources: curriculum textbooks and guides, publishers' scope and sequence charts, teachers' handbooks accompanying basal texts, competency level booklets. With this information and knowledge, the teacher can then set up his own check-list of skills for his particular group of children. Copies of the check-lists may be made so that each child's progress may be observed, evaluated and recorded. The check-list should help the teacher design activity or learning centers that promote overall skills, and also to create a specific skill-building activity when needed.

One caution: don't let the check-list determine the program; let children's needs determine the program. The list is the backbone, the guide. Branch out from it as interests change and as new abilities are acquired.

The sample check-list on pages 34-45 was developed by a second grade teacher for her language arts program.

In Conclusion

The philosophy of the learning-centered classroom presented here may have great appeal for you, and yet you may hesitate in fear that you wouldn't know how to implement it. Let me reassure you, you can do it; any teacher who believes in it can do it. And you will find it easier and easier as you go along, and as you are sparked by your own and your pupils' enthusiasm and success.

In the remaining chapters of this book I will describe specifically and in detail many of the practical things you will need to know in order to organize and develop your own learning-centered classroom. You will find it is easier than you anticipated. Just remember you do not have to make the changeover all at once; you can do it as gradually as is necessary and comfortable.

LANGUAGE ARTS

GRADE 2

PUPIL'S NAME _____

I. Oral Language Development (Comprehension and Use)	DATES PUPIL WAS OBSERVED	CONFERENCE DATES
A. Conversation (Vocabulary, Fluency, Clarity)		
B. Discussion, Opinion, Reaction		
C. Dramatic Presentation		
D. Story Telling		
E. Oral Reading		
F. Poetry		
G. Selecting Facts		
H. Remembering Sequence		
I. Following Directions		
J. Drawing Inferences		
K. Assimilation of Phrases and Idiomatic Meanings		
L. Auditory Discrimination: 1. Initial Sounds 2. Final Sounds 3. Short and Long Vowels 4. Blends 5. Rhyming Words		

°Adapted from a check-list developed by Jill Gefvert, Walnut Elementary School, William Penn School District, Darby, Pa.

CHECK-LIST*

DATES PUPIL WAS TESTED	DATE PUPIL SHOWED MASTERY	COMMENTS

LANGUAGE ARTS

GRADE 2

PUPIL'S NAME _____

II. Reading Development	DATES PUPIL WAS OBSERVED	CONFERENCE DATES
A. Visual Discrimination: 1. Of Letters 2. Use of Picture and Context Clues		
B. Phonic Analysis: 1. Consonants in any Position 2. Short Vowels 3. Long Vowels and Diphthongs 4. Rhyming		
C. Structural Analysis: 1. Rootwords 2. Prefixes 3. Inflectional Endings 4. Contractions 5. Possessives 6. Compound Words 7. Syllabication		
D. Expanding Sight Vocabulary: 1. Content Words 2. Prepositions 3. Conjunctions and Exclamations		

CHECK-LIST

DATES PUPIL WAS TESTED	DATE PUPIL SHOWED MASTERY	COMMENTS

LANGUAGE ARTS

GRADE 2

PUPIL'S NAME _____

II. Reading Development (cont.)	DATES PUPIL WAS OBSERVED	CONFERENCE DATES
4. Personal and Relative Pronouns E. Comprehension: 1. Information, Facts, Details 2. Directions or Procedures 3. Sequence 4. Main Idea 5. Inferences		
III. Written Language Development		
A. Length of Sentences		
B. Complexity (Use of Phrases, Clauses)		
C. Correct Tenses		
D. Use of Pronouns		
E. Agreement (Subject-Verb, Number, Modifiers)		
F. Spelling		
G. Handwriting		

CHECK-LIST

DATES PUPIL WAS TESTED	DATE PUPIL SHOWED MASTERY	COMMENTS

LANGUAGE ARTS

GRADE 2

PUPIL'S NAME _____

III. Written Language Development (cont.)	DATES PUPIL WAS OBSERVED	CONFERENCE DATES
H. Capitalization: 1. To Begin Sentences 2. Proper Nouns		
I. Punctuation: 1. Sentence Endings 2. Commas, Colons and Quotes		
J. Paragraphing: 1. One Idea to a Paragraph 2. Sequence		
K. Story Structure: 1. Opening with Interest 2. Middle (Plot Development) 3. End (Climax, Solution or Final Statement)		
L. Plays: 1. Situation 2. Characters 3. Dialogue 4. Stage Directions		
M. Poetry: 1. Rhyming Verse		

CHECK-LIST

DATES PUPIL WAS TESTED	DATE PUPIL SHOWED MASTERY	COMMENTS

LANGUAGE ARTS

GRADE 2

PUPIL'S NAME _____

III. Written Language Development (cont.)	DATES PUPIL WAS OBSERVED	CONFERENCE DATES
2. Quick Couplets 3. Haiku 4. Cinquains		

N. Other Types of Writing:
1. Summary
2. Book Review
3. Outline
4. Letters
5. Diary
6. Jokes, Riddles, Puzzles
7. News
8. Editorial:
   a. Opinion
   b. Description		

IV. Vocabulary Development		
A. Word Pairs: 1. Antonyms 2. Synonyms 3. Homonyms 4. Multiple Meanings		
B. Word Usage: 1. Abstract Nouns 2. Participles 3. Modifiers		

CHECK-LIST

DATES PUPIL WAS TESTED	DATE PUPIL SHOWED MASTERY	COMMENTS

LANGUAGE ARTS

GRADE 2

PUPIL'S NAME _____

V. Reference Skills	DATES PUPIL WAS OBSERVED	CONFERENCE DATES
A. Alphabetical Order: 1. Using First Two Letters 2. Relating Sound and Letter		
B. Dictionary: 1. Word Meanings 2. Word Pronunciations 3. Other Information (Syllabication, Part of Speech, etc.)		
C. Encyclopedia, Almanac: 1. Knowing Topic Word 2. Using Headings 3. Skimming for Facts 4. Note Taking		
D. Library: 1. Using Card Catalogue 2. Locating Books 3. Using Index & Table of Contents		

CHECK-LIST

DATES PUPIL WAS TESTED	DATE PUPIL SHOWED MASTERY	COMMENTS

III

How to Create a Learning Center

A learning center should not only be appealing and beautiful, with excellent content, but it should also be educationally sound. Centers should not be created haphazardly. They must be developed with specific knowledge in mind, and with a plan that makes learning exciting and allows children to learn more than they would otherwise. If not, the whole learning-centered movement may become just a passing fad that will soon disappear.

This chapter will present the concepts and strategies you need to know in order to gain intellectual satisfaction from making centers that are truly effective.

Procedure for Developing a Center

Each person functions differently; your procedure may be different from my procedure, but it is important that each of us follows a regular procedure. There is plenty of room for variation within the process, but if the teacher does not follow an overall plan fairly consistently, there is the possibility that important elements may be overlooked.

The step-by-step plan presented here may be varied in any way, but the important thing is that you come up with a process that you can use with confidence and with ease.

Steps in Developing Learning Centers

1. Identify an idea
   a. from your own classroom experience or inspiration;
   b. from someone else;
   c. from sample centers you have seen;
   d. from professional books on learning centers;
   e. from other books.

2. Adapt it to needs of your children.
   a. Examine your diagnostic data. (Is the idea needed; is it of interest?)
   b. How much previous exposure, experience is necessary?
   c. Decide whether its purpose is interest or skill.
   d. Define your objective.
   e. Determine appropriate levels.
   f. Decide whether it should be compulsory or non-compulsory.

3. Make the center. (See suggestions that follow.)

4. Place it in the room.

5. Explain it to the class.

Parts of a Center

Each center has a different appearance, but there are basic parts that should be contained in every center. Arrange them within the center to suit your own style.

1. NAME

The name should indicate something about the content of the center, but it should also be catchy enough to attract attention.

The teacher may identify the center by the learning skill involved, but the title the children see focuses on the activity. For example, one of the sample centers in this book is labeled *Classification* in the teacher's directions, but the center is named *It's Moving Day*.

The teacher may also want to number each center for recording and reporting purposes.

If it is the kind of center where the children physically engage in the activity right in the center itself, the teacher will want to post the number of pupils allowed in the center at one time.

2. OBJECTIVE

It is important that children know why they are doing something. Start the habit of making children aware of objectives as early as kindergarten. In writing objectives, keep them short, use clear language, and confine them to about one or two per center.

3. MATERIALS

List any books, equipment or consumable materials children will need. Instill the habit of getting the necessary materials together before starting to work at the center.

4. TASKS

This is the heart of the center. Activities at different levels may be included. The directions should be very clear, and presented one step at a time. The reading level of the children should be considered and the vocabulary and sentence structure of the directions should not present difficulties to the student. Directions should be brief, clear, concise. Use symbols or pictures when needed.

5. EVALUATION

Each center should suggest some means for self-checking. If

the center calls for an answer sheet or a specific system for scoring, this should be included. If there is no way of providing objective checks, some system of feedback should be suggested. For example, in the sample center on poetry *(see page 174)* a method is suggested for getting a subjective response from a fellow student.

Instructions should be included for recording scores (or reactions) for completed work.

6. ON YOUR OWN

Directions should be given for what to do with finished products. Most centers will contain more than one task, at more than one level of difficulty. In addition, there should be suggestions for other similar projects that interested students may undertake.

Sample Center

The sample center on page 50 illustrates briefly the major parts of a learning center.

Independent Worksheets vs. Learning Centers

Many times activities that go by the name of learning centers are actually little more than worksheets. The teacher who has had little training or experience in the creation and use of learning centers sometimes assumes that if he creates worksheets that children can choose or be assigned to work at independently, he has created learning centers. This is not so. Such activities may be very valuable and have an important place in the curriculum, but they should be distinguished from learning centered activities.

Worksheets for independent activities are primarily used for reinforcement or enrichment. They do not usually have objectives stated for the student, or built-in feedback for self-evaluation. They are usually one-shot activities, and the student

NUMBER OF CENTER	NAME OF CENTER	NUMBER OF CHILDREN WHO CAN WORK AT THE CENTER
12	*Big Green What?*	3

Objective

To create a scary object and write an imaginary story about it.

Materials

Paper, pencil, clay, crepe paper, papier-mache, crayons, paint.

Directions

1. Make something green and scary. Use the art materials at this center.

2. Finish this sentence and write the story:

"Nobody knew how it got into the room,
but there it was, a big green _____."

Evaluation

1. Hide the green, scary thing you made behind your back and then suddenly produce it for one of your classmates. What was the reaction?

2. Post your story on the "Big Green?" bulletin board. Put your object on the table under the bulletin board. We will have a contest to choose the scariest object and story.

On Your Own

1. Convert your story into a poem.

2. Convert your story into a play. Choose a cast, rehearse them, and present your performance for the class.

can generally complete them in a very short time. Worksheets tend to concentrate on an isolated task rather than developing an overall skill or concept. (For example: Write 10 words that contain three syllables.)

This is not to say that worksheets are bad or should not be used. Children generally enjoy doing them and profit from the opportunity they offer for practice, reinforcement and a change of pace from group work. But the teacher should not spend too much time making them. Commercial materials in the form of workbooks, ditto sheets, activity cards are readily available. The teacher should avail himself of these and save time for using his creative efforts in making learning centers.

Learning centers consist of a group of tasks arranged in a hierarchical order leading to the acquisition of an ability or the understanding of a concept. For example, the sample presented called "Big Green What?" may be a simple, independent worksheet if it is just one isolated activity in composition writing. On the other hand, if the teacher has an overall plan for the promotion of creative writing, this activity may be one in a series of writing tasks designed to help children develop the ability to write imaginatively, humorously, creatively in various prose and poetry forms. Then it would be one of the stations in a learning center.

Centers vary infinitely in their content and in their design. But the teacher who learns the strategy for creating a learning center gains a systematic approach that enables him to generate ideas that consistently produce learning centers that really teach. There is an art and a science to writing tasks for a learning center. The teacher who has no particular strategy may create some wonderful centers now and then, but he will find the work difficult and time consuming. Learning the strategy makes the work easier and produces more satisfying results more consistently.

Strategy for Developing Learning Centers

There is no special mystique about creating learning centers.

The teacher doesn't have to be wildly creative or artistic. The strategy for creating learning centers simply follows the principles of learning. Any teacher who understands children and who knows the component skills in the various subject areas can master the strategy.

The strategy recognizes that children pass through developmental stages in their social and intellectual growth. It therefore provides for developmentally appropriate tasks by including beginning, continuing and culminating levels of activities. It allows children to move from receptive understanding of concepts to expressive or creative use. Children develop skills and concepts first through sensory activities that are directly experiential (touching, smelling, tasting, cutting, manipulating). They may then use their perceptual abilities in tasks that enable them to apply the skill or concept (matching, comparing, sorting). And at the conceptual and cognitive level, activities are provided that allow the student to extend the skill or concept acquired (generalizing, judging, forming opinions, predicting, creating).

In other words, the strategy for creating learning centers follows the axioms of good teaching by allowing children to move from the simple, concrete, known, to the more complex, abstract, unknown. The chart on the opposite page outlines the sequence of activities to be included in creating a learning center. The activities are necessarily generalized, but once the teacher grasps the essence, he should have little difficulty translating these general skills into specific tasks related to the particular learning center he is developing.

The sample center on rhyming (see page 55) illustrates the strategy of breaking down tasks for a learning center. (The designation of the three levels—beginning, continuing, and culminating—would not appear on the center in the classroom.) The center is not complete, but is designed primarily to show the breakdown of tasks, and includes only part of the directions and some sample activities.

Strategy for Developing Learning Centers[1]		
LEVEL	MAIN TASK	SUGGESTED ACTIVITIES
Beginning	Developing	Manipulating—cutting, matching, pasting, tracing Experimenting—observing, keeping a log, charting, surveying, measuring, counting Listening—audio tapes, records Viewing—filmstrips, slides, film, loops, pictures Discussing, identifying
Continuing	Applying	Filling in Arranging in order Putting together, taking apart Picking out Classifying, sorting Locating Writing, recording, labeling
Culminating	Extending	Comparing Reconstructing Researching, interviewing Deciding if Drawing conclusions, inferences, and generalizations Correlating Inventing, developing your own Trying out Evaluating Using multi-media materials to present work—slides, radio or TV show, audio tape with appropriate music, discussions, debates, drama

1 Parts of this strategy are based on the work of Kaplan, Sandra Nina, et al, *Change for Children*, Pacific Palisades, Calif., Goodyear Publishing Co., Inc., 1973, pp. 21-22; and Don, Sue, et al, *Individualizing Reading with Learning Stations and Centers*, Evansville, Ind., Riverside Learning Associates, Inc., 1974, pp. 8-12.

You will note that a center is made up of *stations*. Any number of stations may be included in a center at each level. Perhaps you would think of other activities you would want to include at one or more levels or stations. The range and depth of the activities depend upon the amount of direct teaching of rhyming you have already done, and on the children's understanding of rhyming. You might decide that your children have had little experience with rhyming and that your centers should include activities only at the beginning level. On the other hand, you might know that your children have a solid understanding of rhyming already and that activities at the first two levels would be completely unchallenging. In this case you would include in your center only activities at the culminating level. Ultimately, tasks should have been provided at all three levels. But you begin where your children are. Keeping records will assure that you, or the next teacher, knows what each child has had and may need next.

This center could easily be made to look interesting and appealing. One way would be to place it on a sheet of colored posterboard. With a flair pen, write the tasks for each station on separate pieces of oaktag or construction paper and arrange them esthetically on the posterboard. You could add pictures of poets, selections of poems or songs and appropriate illustrations.

Another suggestion is to obtain a cardboard box, color or cover it, mount a task on each side of the box so that children work around the box in progressive order according to the stations. Be sure to include any books or materials needed for the center.

Learning centers require a good bit of thought and work (especially initially) by the teacher. But if you make centers like this, you will find that they challenge children and give them more in-depth learning experiences. Eventually, you will have to make fewer centers because this type of task absorbs children for longer periods of time. Also, one activity inevitably leads to others initiated by you or by the children themselves. Soon you will find you are doing less direct teaching and more guiding and stimulating.

Rhyming Time

Objective
To identify words that rhyme.

Materials
Paper, pencil, tape recorder, encyclopedia.

Directions

Station 1   [BEGINNING]

1. Listen to the poem "Trees" on the tape recorder.
   Did you like the poem?
   Listen to it again, and this time pick out all the words
   that rhyme. Write them on a piece of paper.

2. Take a worksheet from the "Rhymes A" pocket.
   (The following is a sampling of the worksheet:)
   Draw a line from each word to the picture that rhymes
   with the word.

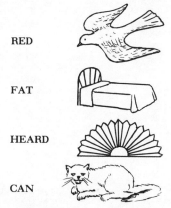

RED

FAT

HEARD

CAN

3. Take a worksheet from the "Rhymes B" pocket.
   (The following is a sampling of the worksheet:)
   Next to each pair of words, write YES if they rhyme.
   Write NO if they do not rhyme.

pale	nail	_____
soap	rope	_____
wool	pool	_____
said	head	_____

Station 2   [CONTINUING]

1. Complete the couplet by filling in the missing rhyming word.

   There once was a man who loved beer,
   He'd drink it each day of the _____.

   My sister married a funny guy,
   He's as bald as an egg, and stands a mile _____.

   Never is there a wind that blows
   As much or as hard as does my _____.

   Draw illustrations for these couplets.

2. List all the words you can think of that rhyme with *ball*.

3. Arrange these words in rhyming groups:

   hear
   fair
   deer
   repair
   there
   mere
   pier
   clear
   declare
   their
   pear
   stare

Station 3   [CULMINATING]

1. Write as many words as you can think of that rhyme with *my*. How many different ways was this vowel spelled in your words? (You should have at least four different spelling groups.)

2. Read some limericks in the books at this center. Choose the one you like best and write it out. Try to paraphrase it to produce your own limerick.

3. Choose a common nursery rhyme, such as *Twinkle, Twinkle, Little Star* or *Little Boy Blue*. Rewrite it so that it says something about your school life. (You may use a rock song, or any other rhyme you like.)

4. Look up the life of Joyce Kilmer in the encyclopedia at this center. Under these headings, write down the facts you find about him: Life   Education   Work

Teachers will use the strategy outlined here in different ways. It depends on the teacher's experience with center teaching. It depends, too, on the grade level. Young children require simpler tasks, one at a time. In the lower grades, then, the centers would be less complex.

It also depends on the children's learning abilities. If you teach average and bright children, the centers will have numerous, varied, and open-ended activities. Slower children, like young children, cannot handle many tasks at one time.

Finally, it depends on children's experience with centers. If you are very experienced with centers, but your children are inexperienced, go slowly. The children need time to learn to work systematically and independently. My own experience has shown that children learn the approach rather quickly. Working at independent activities prepares the way for working at learning centers. Soon you will work out the desired balance between these two types of work, as well as the proportion of direct teaching you will be doing.

Types of Centers

Learning centers vary not only in content but also in purpose. Among the ways to differentiate them are the following:

SKILL VS. INTEREST CENTERS

Skill Centers are designed to give practice in particular skills, such as fractions, vowels sounds, map reading, and such.

Interest Centers capitalize on topics of current interest to children, or attempt to stimulate new interests. They furnish enrichment and provide a change of pace through activities, such as cooking a Japanese meal, making an animated cartoon.

COMPULSORY VS. NON-COMPULSORY CENTERS

Compulsory centers are required of everyone, or of designated children who need practice on the work provided in the center. Skill centers are usually compulsory.

Non-compulsory Centers are there for anyone who wants to take advantage of them. Although the work in these enrichment centers is generally more complex than in the skill centers, children are attracted to them for their stimulating content.

SHORT TERM VS. LONG TERM CENTERS

Short Term Centers exhaust their usefulness when the skill for which they provide practice has been mastered or when interest in the activity wanes. They then come down and may be discarded or stored.

Long Term Centers are continuously expandable as the area is probed in ever greater depth and new materials and activities are added. A center on amphibians or on poetry, for example, might continue for months as various facets of study are added.

All these types of centers will eventually be included in the learning-centered classroom. As the teacher observes the children's participation in the various centers he is alerted to the need to alter, add to or abandon a center as indicated.

Principles for Developing Appealing Centers

Many hints for developing centers have been indicated already. The following reminders highlight some of the main ingredients of successful centers.

1. Gear the content of centers to the needs, abilities, and interests of the class.

2. Make the center colorful and visually appealing so that it attracts children's attention and whets their curiosity. Make it such an exciting place that they will want to come to it.

3. Make use of multi-media materials—slides, filmstrips, audiotapes, film loops, records, cameras, and such.

4. Provide manipulative materials for discovery and exploration whenever possible.

5. Make as many things as you can for your centers yourself. Although commercially prepared materials should also be used, colorful writing, printing, and drawing by the teacher is more personal.

6. Give the centers clever titles, e.g. "Oppomonsters" is more inviting than simply "Opposite Words."

7. Provide a wide variety of activities that range from simple to difficult and concrete to abstract.

8. Gear the tasks so that they will challenge children, but will also give them a chance for success.

9. Make the directions very clear.

10. Try to provide some means for self-checking for each center.

Time Saver Hints

Preparing centers takes time, and for busy teachers time is a luxury. Experience has shown a number of short cuts or time saving ideas that can considerably reduce the work involved in making centers. See if these ideas will work for you.

1. Before making a center, clearly decide upon your goal. Is it to be an independent activity or a true learning center? Is it to be a skill development center or an interest center? Is it to be compulsory or non-compulsory?

2. You don't have to be an artist to make good centers. Use pictures and designs, and lots of color. Cover large boxes with colorful paper or paint them to enhance your center. If you're not adept at art work, perhaps you might find a pupil who is.

3. Don't spend too much time making it artistically accurate. Make your center as attractive as you can, but be prepared to change it if the children don't respond to it.

4. Examine available commercial centers to determine if they can be adapted for use in your classroom. For example, the Instructo Corporation, Paoli, Pa. is marketing learning centers.

5. Use any commercial and "junk" materials that are appropriate.

6. Build up a collection of pictures, words, stories from newspapers, magazines, old textbooks, and old workbooks. Organize these materials so that you can locate items needed for centers.

7. Use your bulletin boards for mounting centers. This eliminates needing to decorate bulletin boards.

8. Use drapery hooks to stick through cardboard or posterboard of your center if you need to attach objects. These are very inexpensive and can be inserted very easily.

9. Attach an eyelet or a grommet to the center and hang over

matching nails, screws, or hooks attached to the wall or bulletin board.

10. Number (or color) code centers and their answer sheets.

11. For centers that have a number of manipulative parts, color code the materials so that if pieces become scattered it will be easy to find where they belong. At each center, record the number of pieces (cards, pictures, puzzle parts, etc.) that belong to it.

12. Use the product *velcro*, which you can purchase in a sewing shop, if you need to stick two surfaces together temporarily. For example, if cards with words are to be matched with cards with pictures, glue a piece of velcro to the front side of one card and another piece to the back side of the other card. The matched cards will hold tightly but can easily be separated.

13. Make an inexpensive acetate folder (for holding material such as a poem, picture or map) by placing two acetate or transparency sheets together and sealing the sides and bottom with masking or scotch tape.

14. Use clear acetate placed over a worksheet for children to write their answers upon. After the answers have been checked, wipe the sheet clean with a sponge or paper towel. If the acetate becomes smudged from many usings, wipe it clean with a piece of scrap carpeting.

15. Change centers frequently, but only one or two at a time, not all at once.

16. Make some centers in which the content may be changed to form a new center, but the background and art work can remain the same. For example, you might have a

creative writing center, "Bubble Gum Blues," on which there are six bubbles with a story starter on each. You can update the center simply by changing the bubbles. A "Scrambled Eggs" center in which children unscramble words may be upgraded or downgraded by changing the scrambled words in the pocket.

17. Build some of your centers around current events that have captured the children's interest. When the Stanley Cup was won by the Philadelphia Flyers hockey team in the spring of 1974, a teacher I know made a mathematics center entitled "Go Flyers Go!" She took a picture of the Flyers that appeared in the local newspaper and attached it to a piece of posterboard. She then mounted mathematics problems to the board based on the picture. For example, "Multiply the number of Flyers' emblems in row 2 by the number of men whose neckties you can see." "Add the number of men in rows 1, 2, and 3; divide that sum by the number of men in row 4." "Multiply the number of men whose teeth you can see by the number of men who have smiles on their faces." Needless to say her children went about this center with vigor, scarcely realizing they were practicing mathematics and reading skills.

18. Plan how you are going to store the center at the time you make it.

19. Don't be afraid to ask for help from colleagues and friends. The sharing of information and materials is a subsidiary benefit of the learning-centered movement.

20. Set up a lending library for centers in your school.

21. Let children help make centers. It is a good thinking,

organizing, and writing activity, one that really challenges children's abilities.

22. Encourage upper grade children to go to lower grade rooms to make centers.

23. Enlist parents and aides to help make centers. Many parents want to visit school but they frequently do not know what to do when they get there. They will enjoy making centers.

IV

Choosing a Model

Deciding what kind of learning center you would like to model your classroom on is very much like buying an automobile. There are many choices open to you when you go out to buy a car—the make, body style, size of motor, number of doors, interior decor, color, optional equipment, and so on. But regardless of what car you decide to purchase, they all have certain commonalities, such as wheels, engines, ignition, glass windows, windshield wipers, brakes, steering wheels, head lights.

There is no one model which is best. Everyone has to choose his own, because we differ in such matters as personality, experience, philosophy, needs, and contingencies. With a learning center model, as with a car, you may want to trade your model in after some time.

Let's go shopping and look at some models.

MODEL 1   The Volkswagen Model

This very simple model makes an excellent introduction to learning-centered education for teachers or children who are new to the experience. It requires very little change in the program or in the physical arrangement of the classroom.

This model starts with one curriculum area—reading, for example. Place a table somewhere in the room where there is easy access to it without impinging on the rest of the classroom. On the table, set up several activities using the learning center format. Show children around the area explaining each activity and the procedures to follow in working there. Allow children to examine the materials and to ask any questions they want.

Do not schedule specific times for children to use the learning center. Simply encourage children to try it when they have finished tasks that the rest of the group is still working on. As you get to know your children, you will know which ones work fast in which areas and you will be able to vary your group work to provide opportunities for each child to be free to wander and work in the learning center.

This is a viable model which is very easily organized. It generally furnishes teachers and children with a satisfying initial experience with the learning-centered classroom, making it possible to move on gradually to more sophisticated models.

MODEL 2   The Super Beetle Model

This model is still restricted to one curriculum area, but it incorporates the learning center into the regular school program. The teacher creates a number of activities or centers, each clearly labeled and numbered. At the very beginning, the teacher may decide to schedule only part of the class to work at these activities in order to start out with those children who seem to be able to work independently. They may be scheduled to work at the learning center for a short period several times a week at first. Children are assigned to specific activities in the center to begin with. A daily schedule of assignments is posted.

Gradually, the length of time, the number of days, and the number of children working at the activities in the learning center increase. Until they become quite familiar with the procedures, a daily schedule is posted assigning children to specific activities. The teacher should provide enough activities so that no more than four children are working at a particular center at the same time. The assignments should be changed as

Center Assignments,			
SYNONYM RUMMY	ANTONYM CONCENTRATION	SPELLING FUN	LONG FORMS AND SHORT FORMS
Billy	Betty	Jan	Dick
Don	Chip	Jerry	Dot
Mary	Genie	John	Helen
Sue	Judy	Pat	Nick

the teacher observes the children's progress.

The daily schedule can be in chart form. Or, for variety, the teacher may write each child's name on a clothespin and clip no more than four clothespins to each center.

Still another variation is to stretch a line across part of the room, hanging the numbers of the learning centers on it and attaching clothespins to each number showing where each child is to work.

MODEL 3   The Chevrolet or Ford Model

In this model, there is quite a dramatic change in the physical arrangement of the room. Centers are scattered about in various

February 16, 1:30-2:00

PHONICS FUN	COMPREHENSION MAGIC	SOUND ALIKES
Kathie	Alex	Denise
Linda	Cheryll	George
Rick	Ellen	José
Steve	Lloyd	Sarah

parts of the room, using imagination to find unusual materials, schemes, and locations for displaying them. Considerably more movement is permitted the children in this model and a great deal more space is used.

The following diagram shows some of the possible ways for arranging centers. The traditional, formal arrangement of furniture in neat rows, and the conventional desks are, for the most part, replaced by free or inexpensive, easily obtainable materials, making for more interesting interior decoration.

Not all these ideas will appear in a single classroom. The teacher will select suggestions that fit his room and his style. What the diagram shows is that with a little imagination and ingenuity, space, even small space, can be interestingly and effectively used.

MODEL 3 CLASSROOM

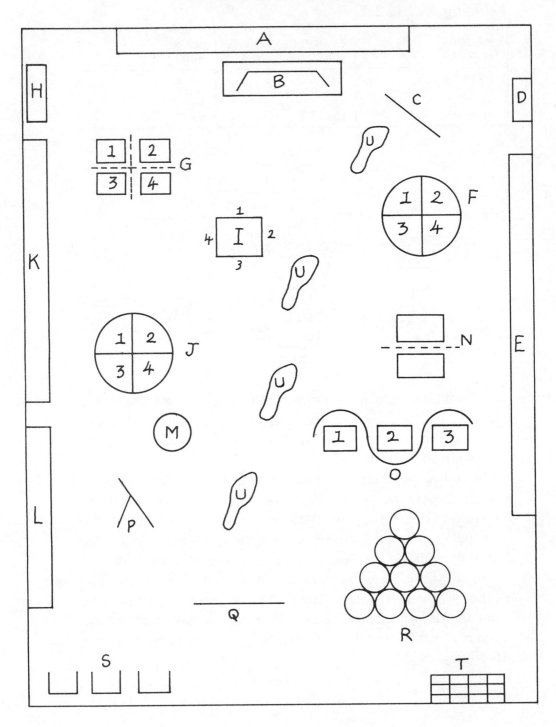

LEGEND FOR MODEL 3

A Under the chalkboard: In many classrooms there is an area between the chalkboard and the floor that is usually unused. Centers that are made of posterboard or similar materials may have grommets or eyelet holes placed in the upper corners and may be hung over matching nails or screws attached to the wall. Children may remove these centers to work upon elsewhere, or they may sit on the floor in front of them.

B On the desk or table: Find a rather large cardboard box. Cut out the top, bottom, and one side. Form a screen of the three remaining sides and place it on a desk or table. The three sides may provide space for three centers, or for one center that progresses from one level to another.

C Divider: Portable dividers mounted on pedestals or rollers provide a front and back surface for mounting centers.

D Closet or locker door: Most rooms have several doors in them. Attach centers to these.

E Chalkboard tray: Stand small centers that are in envelopes or folders in the chalkboard tray.

F Table with dividers: Create dividers of plywood, masonite, tri-wall, hardboard or other substances to fit an available round, square or rectangular table. Space for four centers is made available in this way.

G Desks with dividers: Instead of a table, four pupils' desks may be tied together, and dividers which stand on the floor may be made as described in F.

H Crate: Not all centers need to be large. Small centers that are interesting and challenging can be made and placed in manilla envelopes. One crate or box might be a treasure chest that holds as many as 50 centers.

I Cardboard Box: A rather large cardboard box that once held a TV, range or refrigerator may be painted or covered with contact paper. The four sides then provide space for different centers, or for one center that progresses from one level to the other.

J Electric cable spool: An electric cable spool can serve as a table and dividers can be made for it as described in F.

K Window sill: If it is wide enough, centers in envelopes or folders may be laid along the window sill.

L Bulletin board: Use any available bulletin boards for mounting centers.

M Lampshade: Obtain a rather large old lampshade. Place it on a table or on the floor and mount centers all around the sides.

N Desks: Tie two pupil desks together and place a divider between them to make space for two centers.

O Desks: Using three or four pupil desks, weave corrugated paper between them to make private nooks for centers.

P Easel: Mount a center to an available easel.

Q Cloth divider from ceiling: Suspend a divider made of fabric (burlap or an old sheet or tablecloth) from the ceiling. Mount wooden strips or dowels at the top and bottom to make it more steady. Attach centers to both sides.

R Empty ice-cream cartons: Large round ice-cream cartons may be obtained from Baskin-Robbins or Carvel and glued together in pyramids. Small centers may be housed in envelopes or folders in these cartons, or they may be used for completed paper.

S Large boxes: Obtain several boxes large enough for a child to get inside. Cut out the front side and place a pad in the bottom. Let children get inside them to complete center tasks, read, or do other quiet activities.

T Mail box of milk cartons or shoe boxes: To provide a place for returning papers, contracts, leaving messages and such, obtain half-gallon milk cartons, color them, and staple them together in a tier arrangement. The same end may be accomplished by using liquor or wine cartons with the bottle partitions forming a cubby hole mailbox.

U Footprints: Make footprints of cardboard, rug scraps, or such. Using masking tape, attach word strips to them which invite interest in a given highlight of the room. For example, "This way for a special exhibit."

MODEL 4   The Buick Model

In this model, children are given a choice about which centers to work on. It is desirable to move to this stage as early as feasible because it is here that children develop independence, one of the big aims of learning-centered teaching.

Experience has shown that children need and enjoy being given choices and making decisions for themselves. It is a mistake to assign them to centers for too long. The sooner you can move to the choice stage the better, but be sure you are ready and the children are able to work more independently.

The physical arrangement of the room and the amount of time spent at learning center activities are determined by the teacher, but children are now given options about where they will work.

If children are to make a choice of centers, you need to develop some system for them to declare their choice. One method is to have a contract form upon which they declare which centers they plan to work in. This may be a daily or a weekly form, depending upon the stage both you and they are in.

A sample daily form is presented here. Others appear in the Appendix. After the child completes the form, he brings it to the teacher, who initials it. The child keeps it with him; when finished he gives it to the teacher along with the work he has completed for the day.

DAILY CONTRACT FORM

Name _____

Date _____

I will complete centers numbered as follows:

_____   _____

_____   _____

_____   _____

Teacher's Initials _____

Another method for having children register their choices is to use the chart on page 72, or the clothesline, page 66. Only this time, instead of the teacher assigning children to centers, the children choose their own and post or hang their names where they wish. As they complete one center, they remove their name and hang it where they will be working next. This has the advantage of giving the teacher a bird's-eye view of where each child is at any given time, and it also automatically limits the number of children that are in the same center at the same time. Other suggestions will be found in Chapter 6, Managing the Classroom.

MODEL 5 The Two-Car Owner Model

In this model, you move into additional curriculum areas. If

	BOB	MARY	JOHN	SUE
1 Synonym Rummy				
2 Antonym Concentration				
3 Spelling Fun				
4 Long Forms and Short Forms				
5 Phonics Fun				
6 Comprehension Magic				
7 Sound Alikes				

you have started with reading and language arts, you might now add mathematics. As soon as this area is working smoothly, move into still another area. Gradually learning-centered activities will be extended to include all curriculum areas.

MODEL 6 The Cadillac Model Complete with Television, Bar, and Two Telephones

In this model, you change your program and the physical arrangement of the room dramatically. You concentrate your centers so that they are grouped by curriculum areas or areas of study. A typical room might have a mathematics center, reading center, science center, social studies center, dramatics center, creative writing center, sewing center, construction center, and, so on commensurate with the age and needs of your children.

Get rid of most of the pupil desks; a child's home base is the entire classroom rather than one specific point. Increase the amount of time spent daily on centers. Retain enough direct teaching to meet the needs of small groups. Use large group instruction whenever it is necessary or expedient (for example, to introduce new materials or explain new procedures).

This model most closely approximates the British Integrated Day or the open education model. It is an error to make this model the initial, or even final, objective of the learning-centered classroom. Start with some of the simpler models, moving along only if and when you and the children are ready. There are gains to be enjoyed in the process itself; there is no final goal; each step is a goal in itself.

The models suggested are just that—models. There is nothing magical about the six described here; numerous others could be conceived. Parts of the suggested models can be easily inter-changed. For example, some teachers start contracting earlier than Model 4; some skip Models 1 and 2 and start with Model 3; others use Model 5 before Model 4. The determining factors are the teacher's commitment to the whole process, the children's readiness for independent work, and parental acceptance of the more open methods. Teachers need the freedom to start wherever they feel comfortable and to progress as far as they want to go. Teachers who feel pressured, externally or inter-nally, to use more sophisticated models than they are ready for very likely will not be successful and might abandon the whole learning-centered approach. An administrator may prefer to have every teacher at the same stage, but just as learning centers are designed to meet the individual needs of children, so must the individual differences in teachers be respected, too.

Essential Features of All Models

So, there is no single or ideal model the teacher should pattern his learning-centered classroom on. And the deployment, num-ber, design, content of learning centers may be as varied as there are ideas in teachers' heads, and children with needs and interests to be met. Nevertheless, an observer in learning-centered classrooms would note certain commonalities in theoretical orientation and in methodological approach. These are the motor, brakes, wheels, lights of the car, whatever the model.

1. The teacher understands and believes in the learning-center philosophy of education.

2. The teacher has administrative support for going in this direction.

3. Assessment of pupil needs is the heart of the learning-centered approach.

4. Each center has been conceived and created to meet some perceived interest or need of class members.

5. Each center is more or less self-contained, with a title, number, readily available materials, clear directions, defined goal, suggestions for self-evaluation and for follow-up.

6. The centers have been explained to children and they have an understanding and capability for working independently, alone or with one or more others, to complete activities.

7. The teacher circulates as children work on centers, observing and helping and making mental notes for future use.

8. Everyone starts slowly and moves gradually. Commercial, as well as teacher-made materials may be used. The amount of time allotted to learning centers daily will vary from teacher to teacher, and for one teacher at different stages. Initially children may be assigned to centers; eventually they are given more freedom of choice.

V

Organizing the Classroom

Organizing a learning-centered classroom involves planning for space, movement, time, materials, teaching techniques. The classroom becomes less like a lecture hall and more like a home with people and furnishings placed where they are appropriate, comfortable, accessible and esthetically pleasing.

Space and Movement

If you have a large classroom, you are fortunate and your job is considerably easier. The smaller your classroom, the more planning you have to do. Here are some features to consider.

1. Make purposeful movement legitimate. There's nothing wrong with children moving freely about a room. There *is* something wrong with children's having to sit stock still for a considerable part of the day.

2. Create small groupings (4-6) of children, preferably at tables, or at desks bunched together. This arrangement allows children to ask a neighbor a question, or make a comment or observation, and promotes language and social development. It also sets up a more life-like situation. In real life people ask questions to find answers. The classroom in which children sit separately in straight rows mitigates against this.

3. Form as many flat surfaces as possible in order for children to have sufficient place to spread out materials for working on tasks. These surfaces may be achieved with tables, by grouping desks of the same height together, or by laying a wide board across two desks.

4. Get rid of some of the desks, but not all at one time for children tend to become disoriented. As you eliminate desks, provide places in which children may store their belongings—boxes, cubby holes, tote trays, plastic bins or such. Children do need an accessible place for safekeeping their possessions.

5. Make more use of the floor. Use scatter rugs, benches, pillows, pads, easy chairs, boxes and such. These not only create a more informal atmosphere, but they take up less space than desks and chairs and serve the same purpose.

6. Find other school areas in which children might work, such as hallways, library, lounge, art rooms, outdoors and such. Check them out first to see that they are available for use by your children. Work out rules for using these areas so that children don't abuse the rights of others.

7. Group noisy and quiet areas so that they do not conflict. For example, do not place the dramatics center next to the instructional area. Put painting, science, and messy areas near the sink. Put reading and writing centers in well lighted areas. Let children know which are the quiet and the noisy areas.

Materials

1. Stock a supply table or bin with the commonly used materials—crayons, paper, scissors, rulers, paste. Making

these materials available eliminates many interruptions by pupils in need of supplies.

2. Have a place for everything. Label containers so that everything can be returned to its own place. Teach children the habit of returning materials to their assigned places. Make use of shelves, boxes, cubby holes, desk drawers, envelopes, filing cabinets, or other available storage spaces.

3. Color code materials that go together in one center. This will save you and the children endless hours trying to find where cards, discs, and other miscellaneous items belong if they are found lying about.

4. Provide unusual materials related to what children are studying that will arouse their interest and imagination— bicycle wheels, cocoons, bird nests, rock collections, shells, tree stumps. Use these materials to stimulate discussion, touching, observing, experimenting. Work these materials into centers.

5. Make an effort to make the room look like a workshop rather than a stereotyped classroom.

Teaching Techniques

The role of the teacher changes considerably in a learning-centered environment. From a purely organizational view, the conventional approach, with the teacher holding forth before the entire group, is infinitely easier. The major problem in a learning-centered classroom is to set up the organizational procedures and build up the competencies in children that will enable them to function independently and free the teacher to be a true guide and consultant, able to give each child what he needs. An inexperienced teacher will find this difficult, but with time and patience it can be achieved and the rewards are great. Some practical suggestions are offered here to facilitate this process.

1. Place the teacher's desk in an inconspicuous place, perhaps at the side of the room. This places the teacher in a less authoritative position and connotes that more responsibility and self-reliance are expected from pupils.

2. Keep a daily schedule, developed with the children, on the chalkboard or elsewhere in full view. This procedure lets pupils know what is going on; it sets up orderly learning habits, and aids in evaluation at the end of the day by showing what was and was not accomplished.

3. Post a chart of rules, developed by the students. For example, a typical fifth grade chart might contain the following:

How We Work on Centers

1. Fill in your contract form and show it to the teacher.

2. Plan to do only as much as you will be able to finish.

3. If there are too many others already working at a center you want, go to the next center on your contract.

4. Finish the work at one center before going to another one.

5. Return everything where it belongs.

6. Put your completed work in your folder.

4. Have a signal for quiet that can immediately get everyone's attention if there is a need to. You might use a whistle or a bell, flick the lights, plunk the piano, or such.

5. Provide places to exhibit children's original work. Bulletin boards, clothes-lines stretched across the room, hallways can be used effectively to display children's finished work.

6. Have a book corner with a rug, good lighting and comfortable seating to promote interest and independence in reading. Constructing a loft makes for a good book nook. Bring new books in frequently. Stock current newspapers and magazines.

7. Set up a research corner containing basic research materials—encyclopedia, dictionaries, atlas, thesaurus, and other factual books such as the *Guinness Book of World Records*, guidebooks, how-to books.

Arranging the Classroom

The particular type of room arrangement will be chosen by the teacher in accordance with his organizational and esthetic sense, and dependent upon the stage of learning-centered teaching the class is at. The six models presented in Chapter IV illustrated a gradual transition from a traditional to a learning-centered environment. Any number of alternate arrangements are, of course, possible.

Regardless of the model chosen, certain features should be considered. There should be places where children can work individually, in pairs, or in small groups. Quiet areas should be widely separated from noisy or active areas. Partitions can be strategically placed to provide privacy or shelter from distractions.

An instructional area must be designated where the teacher can work with individuals or small groups or hold conferences. It should be located near a chalkboard and bookshelves, and it would be preferable to have a rug on the floor. The teacher's chair should put him at eye level with the children. The rule should be made that no child may interrupt the teacher when he is working in the instructional center. (Of course exceptions have to be made when emergencies arise.)

To illustrate a few more alternatives for room arrangement, several diagrams are given. Perhaps you can combine selected elements from various models to find one that best suits you.

MODEL 1

Model 1 shows a very simple way to arrange the room, yet very sophisticated teaching and learning can take place. Very few changes from the traditional classroom are needed in order to convert to this model. An instructional area, a listening center, and a book corner are created. The centers (mounted on children's desks or tables) are housed in one part of the room separated from the rest of the room by dividers made of corrugated paper or screens. One group decorated this partition and wrote "206 Hideaway" in large letters on the front of the corrugated divider. Children who showed independence were allowed to go to this area to work for a part of the day. Setting up this special area provided a great incentive for the children to do their work well in order to be allowed to work in the hideaway.

One interesting feature is the "Time Out Area," which can be provided in any model. It is a secluded area equipped with books, independent activities and games, where a child who is having a particularly "hyper" day may spend some time alone. Children understand that they must work here. They may take

MODEL 1

INSTRUCTIONAL
CENTER

LISTENING CENTER

BOOK CORNER

DIVIDER (corrugated paper, screens)

Pupil desks with centers on them

TIME OUT
AREA

Shelves for centers made with boards, bricks

their work with them or use the materials that are there. It takes a child out of the routines of the regular classroom for a while and gives him a chance to work out his tensions.

MODEL 2

In Model 2, which was suggested in the Interning for Learning Project, Cape May County, New Jersey, the room is divided into five distinct areas.

Area I, the Instructional Center, is where direct teaching with small or large groups takes place. Considered a most important part of the classroom, it is located where the teacher can see the entire room, and is "off-bounds" to children not receiving direct instruction.

Area II, the Follow-up Area, is where children go following direct teaching done in Area I. Located in the center of the room, it is made up of pupil desks or tables arranged so that children can help each other complete the follow-up work assigned— ditto sheets, creative work, or work with commercial materials. Children move from Area I directly to Area II to follow-up the direct teaching.

Area III houses the Learning Centers, arranged on pupil desks around the perimeter of the room. Some desks face bulletin boards, doors, or walls upon which centers are mounted. Children are less distracted when seated with their backs to the other activities occurring in the room.

Area IV, the Listening Center, is a quiet area where children listen through earphones to commercial or teacher-made instructional audio tapes. It has been found that if children are assigned to this area for skill work on tapes more than three periods per week they grow tired of it. The center should include enrichment tapes for literature, poetry and music.

MODEL 2*

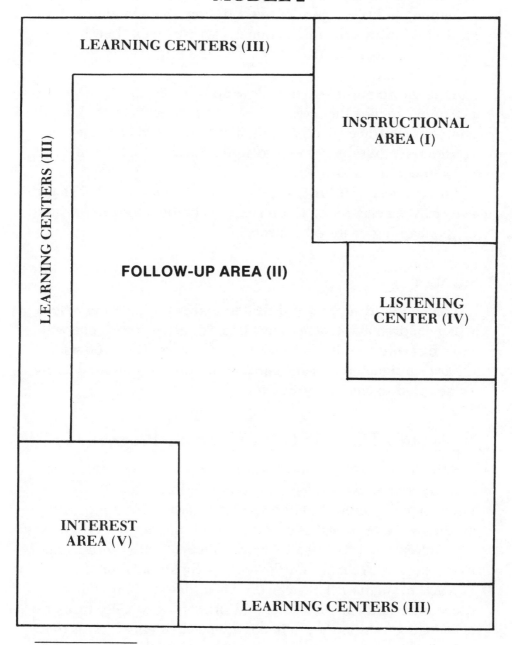

LEARNING CENTERS (III)

LEARNING CENTERS (III)

INSTRUCTIONAL AREA (I)

FOLLOW-UP AREA (II)

LISTENING CENTER (IV)

INTEREST AREA (V)

LEARNING CENTERS (III)

*Title III, Interning for Learning, Cape May County, New Jersey, and Paul Daniels, Johns Hopkins University. Used by permission.

Area V, the Interest Area, consists of free choice activities such as games, hobbies, puzzles, art, drama, bookbinding. It is located as far from the Instructional Area as possible because it is a more noisy area than the others. It is desirable to locate it near a sink if possible.

After they complete their follow-up work in Area II, children may move to the other areas. They may choose where to go and complete contracts to indicate their choices, or when the teacher considers it advisable, he may assign specific children to specific tasks in certain areas.

This is a very viable model, one that calls for limited changes in an existing classroom. It is an excellent model for early stages of the learning-centered approach.

MODEL 3

This model is more sophisticated and is used at later stages when children and teacher have had extensive experience with learning centers in all curricular areas. Centers are placed within the area designated for each curriculum subject. This model can be adapted to suit any grade level.

Integrating Learning Centers into the Program

Both the teacher and the children need a great deal of training and experience before learning centers can become the major instructional medium. Therefore it is advisable to proceed gradually, incorporating one facet at a time into the program.

Children need to learn to work independently without the usual excessive reliance on the teacher for stimulation, instruction and evaluation. They can do this if they start out with easy tasks using familiar materials, and progress gradually to more challenging tasks as they gain confidence in themselves, as they acquire academic and research skills, and as they learn to use each other as learning resources.

MODEL 3

Tables	Tables

READING
AND WRITING

Tables with Reference Books

Tables

MATH

SCIENCE
AND

Bookcase

Supply Table

Bookcase

CLASSROOM
LIBRARY

(with rug and
comfortable seats)

AREA

Sink

WORK

SOCIAL
STUDIES

Teachers Desk

DISPLAY AREA

Individual Storage

PAINTING
AND CRAFTS

Individual Storage

Individual Storage

INSTRUCTIONAL
AREA

Teachers need to learn how to assess their children and how to create learning activities that meet each child's needs and ability level. They can do this if they start out by using commercially available materials, beginning by making appropriate selections, proceeding then to adapt these materials for their own specific purposes and gradually building up to creating their own materials.

Both teacher and children need time to incorporate this new educational approach. Thus, at first only a short segment of school time is allotted to learning centers. This time is extended as it becomes appropriate. Also, at the outset choices are limited, and gradually more and more freedom of choice, activity and movement are enjoyed.

The schedules on page 88 deal with only one hour of the school day and cover only one subject. They illustrate how a gradual transition may be made from traditional teaching to the learning-centered approach. The conventional reading lesson has all children working on the same story in the basal reader at the same time and then doing the same pages in the workbook. These schedules show how direct group teaching may be supplemented by individual independent practice.

In the first stage, only commercially available materials are used, the goals being to encourage children to work independently, and to enable the teacher to make selections of commercial materials that are appropriate for each child.

The class is divided into three reading groups. During the hour devoted to reading, the teacher spends twenty minutes in succession with each of these reading groups, conducting a group lesson in a basal reader or library book or skill builder. The top two groups receive this group instruction only three times a week, freeing the teacher to observe all the children for forty minutes twice a week. The bottom group receives daily group instruction.

During the forty minutes (or sixty minutes twice a week for the two top groups) when they are not receiving direct instruction, the children are given specific assignments in basal readers, workbooks, skill builders, which they complete independently. Each assignment is for twenty minutes.

The room arrangement need not change much. An inviolable instructional area needs to be designated, and the materials to be used by the children need to be placed in assigned areas in the room (shelves, tables, boxes), with children responsible for getting their own specified materials and returning them to their places. Each child is given a schedule of assignments for the day or for the week specifying the materials and pages to be used.

As the children become accustomed to working independently at their individual assignments, and as the teacher gets to know exactly where each child is in reading, the teacher begins to create learning centers that will provide children with needed practice and will stimulate and challenge them. A few such centers are introduced at a time and the children are shown how to work in them. Most likely the teacher will start with the top group. Work in centers is assigned at the beginning, but later on those children who are ready for it may be given free choice.

The number and variety of centers will increase gradually until there is material available suitable for each child. The teacher may also gradually alter the room arrangements making room for work in the centers. In addition to circulating and observing the children at work when he is not doing direct group teaching, the teacher may schedule brief individual conferences with children.

The Stage 2 schedule shows how, at a later stage, work in commercial materials is gradually replaced by work in learning centers created by the teacher with the specific needs of his children in mind.

Scheduling

As has been indicated, there are many different ways to schedule center time. At one end of the spectrum is scheduling no time, but simply placing centers about the room to be used for enrichment. At the other end is extending learning centers

Reading—Stage 1

		MONDAY	TUESDAY	WEDNESDAY	THURSDAY	FRIDAY
9:00- 9:20	Group 1	Group Lesson	Continental Press	Group Lesson	Continental Press	Group Lesson
	Group 2	Barnell Loft	SRA	Reader's Digest	Scholastic Kit	Reader's Digest
	Group 3	Reader's Digest	Barnell Loft	SRA	Scholastic Kit	Continental Press
9:20- 9:40	Group 1	Workbook	Barnell Loft	Workbook	Scholastic Kit	Continental Press
	Group 2	Continental Press	Workbook	SRA	Workbook	Workbook
	Group 3	Group Lesson	Group Lesson	Group Lesson	Group Lesson	Group Lesson
9:40-10:00	Group 1	SRA	Barnell Loft	SRA	Reader's Digest	Scholastic Kit
	Group 2	Group Lesson	Scholastic Kit	Group Lesson	Continental Press	Group Lesson
	Group 3	Workbook	Workbook	Workbook	Workbook	Workbook

Language Arts—Stage 2

		MONDAY	TUESDAY	WEDNESDAY	THURSDAY	FRIDAY
9:00- 9:20	Group 1	Group Lesson	Phonics Center	Group Lesson	Structural Analysis Center	Group Lesson
	Group 2	Phonics Center	Structural Analysis Center	Composi-tion Center	Free Reading	Creative Writing Center
	Group 3	Structural Analysis Center	Study Skills Center	Phonics Center	Literature Center	Composition Center
9:20- 9:40	Group 1	Workbook	Composition Center	Workbook	Study Skills Center	Literature Center
	Group 2	Workbook	Literature Center	Workbook	Composition Center	Study Skills Center
	Group 3	Group Lesson	Group Lesson	Group Lesson	Group Lesson	Group Lesson
9:40-10:00	Group 1	Creative Writing Center	Free Reading	Literature Center	Composition Center	Creative Writing Center
	Group 2	Group Lesson	Phonics Center	Group Lesson	Literature Center	Group Lesson
	Group 3	Workbook	Workbook	Workbook	Workbook	Workbook

into every curriculum area and devoting the entire day to learning centers. In between are arrangements which schedule one or more blocks of time to learning centers in one or more curriculum areas to some or all groups of children.

Schedules not only vary from one teacher to another, but for one teacher at various stages. In fact, scheduling is neither as complicated nor as mysterious as it might seem and the teacher should not hesitate to change his schedule as needed, every day if warranted. It is a good idea to make your children partners in the scheduling task. This not only helps them learn how to organize, but gives them a stake in setting realistic goals. They will gradually learn to make decisions based not only on their wishes but considering reality factors.

The following schedules are included to show that a schedule may be relatively simple. Scheduling should not be the thing that hangs a teacher up from running a learning-centered classroom. Just start with something that seems feasible and keep improving it.

MONDAY, OCTOBER 9

9:00 - 9:30	Class meeting and planning
9:30 - 10:00	Directed reading lesson
10:00 - 10:30	Mathematics
10:30 - 11:40	Language Arts centers
11:40 - 11:50	Clean-up
11:50 - 12:50	Lunch and recess
12:50 - 1:05	Story
1:05 - 1:40	Science (or Social Studies or Gym)
1:40 - 2:30	Language Arts centers
2:30 - 2:40	Clean-up
2:40 - 3:00	Evaluation and planning

Another schedule* might be as follows:

MONDAY, OCTOBER 9				
9:00 - 9:30	Class meeting and planning			
9:30 - 11:30	Language Arts			
	GROUP 1	GROUP 2	GROUP 3	GROUP 4
9:30 - 10:00	Group lesson	Listening Center	Learning Center	Worksheet
10:00 - 10:30	Worksheet	Group lesson	Listening Center	Learning Center
10:30 - 11:00	Learning Center	Worksheet	Group lesson	Listening Center
11:00 - 11:30	Free Choice	Learning Center	Worksheet	Group lesson
11:30 - 12:00	Gym			
12:00 - 1:00	Lunch and free play			
1:00 - 1:20	Story			
1:20 - 2:00	Mathematics			
2:00 - 2:40	Science (or Social Studies)			
2:40 - 3:00	Clean-up, evaluation and planning			

---

*   Adapted from a schedule used by Interning for Learning, Title III, ESEA, Cape May County, New Jersey.

VI

Managing the Classroom

The teacher who treats his class not as a group but as separate and different individuals needs to become a very good organizer and manager. It is much easier to stay on top of things when only one thing is going on at a time. But when learning centers are introduced and children are doing different things in different parts of the room, unless the teacher has a very clear idea of the overall plan, it is easy to become confused or frustrated. Working out simple systems and schedules in advance will prevent this from happening.

In previous chapters, managing the physical setup of the room and arranging schedules of activities were discussed. In this chapter we will consider the deployment of children and of materials.

Assigning Children to Centers

A few suggestions for assigning pupils to centers were given in Chapter IV. Some additional systems are presented here.

1. Make up a board with pockets on it. On each pocket write the number of each center in the room. Make a name strip for each child and insert the name strip in the pocket for the center at which the child is to work.

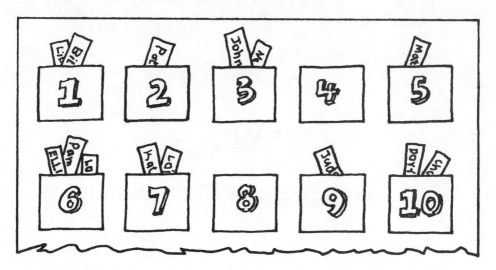

2. A variation is to make up a board with one pocket for each child. Insert in each pocket a strip listing the number(s) of the center in which the child is to work.

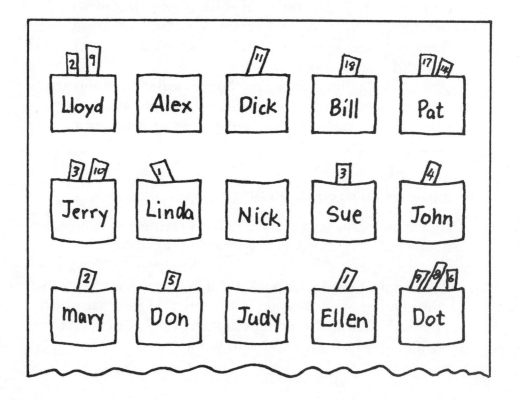

3. When you make up a learning center, mount a pocket on it into which you may insert name strips for children who are to work in the center.

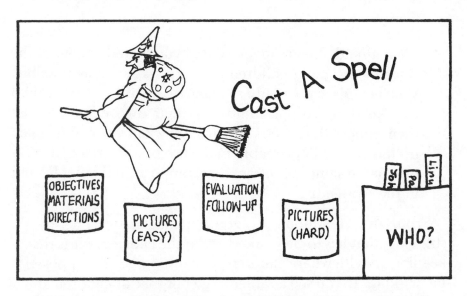

4. Prepare a monthly form listing all the children in the class. Beside each child's name write the number (or numbers) of the center in which he is to work each day. Post this in a prominent place in the classroom.

Learning Center Assignments

FEBRUARY	5	6	7	8	9	12
Jack A.	6	5,9	1	4	2,7	3
Sue A.	9	7,6	4	1	3,8	2
Betty B.	4	3,5	8	2	1,7	6
Chip B.	5	2,8	6	5	7,4	1
Genie B.	1	3,4	2	6	5,9	8
Ellen H.	2	1,7	5	11	6,3	9
Mary L.	11	4,1	7	9	10,2	5
Judy M.	8	5,4	11	10	9,1	6

Instead of using the numbers of the centers on this chart, the name of the center may be listed, or a symbol may be pasted to the center and the same symbol posted on the chart.

5. It has already been suggested that you should get out of the stage of assigning children to centers as soon as possible. When children are ready to make reasonable decisions and to take some responsibility for their own education, let them choose the centers in which they will work. When you do this, you will probably make use of a contract form. A number of sample contract forms appear in Chapter IV and in the Appendix.

From the standpoint of good management, one of the strategies that has to be worked out in the choice stage is that of keeping up with where children are working, or are supposed to be working. If you see a rather large number of children at one center, you can suspect that some of them should not be there. If you see a child doing nothing, you need some way of figuring out where he should be working. If you see children doing something other than working on centers you need some method that tells you where they should be working.

Instead of having to seek out children's contracts, a visual means should be set up for showing where each child is supposed to be working.

One visual method is to get a large piece of pegboard. Divide the board in half with a strip of colored masking or book binding tape. On one side of the board put a peg for each child. Make name tags for all the children and hang them on the pegs. On the other half of the board place a peg for each center with the number of the center written above (or under) the peg. When a child goes to work on a center, he takes his name tag and hangs it on the peg of the center where he is going to work. When he is finished, he moves his name tag to another center. At the end of the session all name tags are returned to the original position.

NAMES					CENTERS				
					1	2	3	4	5
John	Pat	Jack	Lina	CHIP	6	7	8	9	10
Tim	Jerry	Jim	Lotte	Dory	11	12	13	14	15
Tom	Jake	Joe	Ron	Mary	16	17	18	19	20
Jud	Pam	Kim	Tina	Nan	21	22	23	24	25
Kip	Ike	mike	Dena	Dick					

An alternative is to get a large piece of cardboard on which you mount a pocket for each center. Also make a pocket to hold name tags of all the children. The child places his name tag in the pocket of the center at which he is going to work.

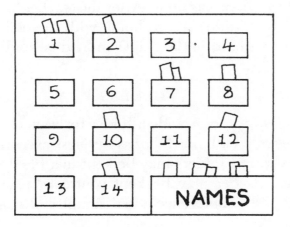

These devices permit the teacher to see at a glance where a given child or children should be. Or, looking at it another way, it is a way for the child to let the teacher know his intention. Thus, the board serves as a kind of contract.

Managing Materials

Some of the materials needed at the center (samples, directions, worksheets) are mounted directly on the center. Others (newspapers, books, maps, equipment) are placed on a table or shelf or in a folder or box near the center. It has already been suggested that these materials be numbered or color coded to prevent loss.

COMPLETED WORK

In addition to whatever self-evaluation techniques are included in the center, it is important that children get feedback from the teacher fairly quickly. A system must be set up for completed work. There might be an envelope or box at each center in which children deposit their completed papers. Or the teacher might provide a "Finished Work Box" in some centrally located place.

The important thing is that the child knows that the teacher will see the work he has done. After the teacher has checked it, the completed work may go home with the child, or it may sometimes be stored in the child's individual folder.

FOLDERS

It is a good idea to provide a folder for each child. Children are as impressed with portfolios as business executives are with attaché cases. The folders may be kept in a file drawer or in a box. In each folder may be kept contracts, planning forms, progress reports, conference notes, samples of completed and checked work.

The folder should be accessible to the teacher and to the child at all times. The teacher will find these folders particularly helpful for parent conferences.

Keeping Notes

Unless the teacher sets up some temporary recording system, he will find it hard to retain the myriads of impressions and observations of individual children that are so useful when planning new learning centers or small group instruction. One way is to keep a packet of index cards handy in your pocket or on your desk. As you circulate among the children and observe their work, jot down cryptic notes to yourself about things you want to follow up. For example: "Trouble with contractions—Billy, John, Sue, Mary, Hazel; form small group." "All children have finished No. 9." "Help John with fractions." "Make a center on inventors." The human mind is a wonderful instrument, but in the hustle and bustle of a busy classroom, it is best not to rely on your memory. The more you can write down the better.

Using Commercial Materials

There are some excellent commercial materials that provide enrichment, follow-up and reinforcement of skills and concepts. If the teacher feels free to select specific items and exercises from among all the materials available, commercial materials can furnish a fine center intermixed with teacher-made materials and other learning centers.

You might have in your classroom these commercial reading materials appropriate to your grade level: SRA Reading Kit, Reading for Understanding cards, Continental Press workbooks, Barnell Loft workbooks, Readers Digest Skill Builders. Specific selections could be assigned to individual children using a form something like this:

NAME: JOHN ROGERS					
Week of	SRA	RFU	Continental Press	Barnell Loft	Readers Digest
Feb. 5-9	1-b Brown 6-15 21/25		Patterns & Usage pp. 11-13 12/15	Following Directions C pp. 16-22 18/26	
Feb. 12-16					
Feb. 19-23					
Feb. 26-Mar. 2					

In the upper half of the box, write the specific assignment of level and pages; in the lower half, record the score showing the number right out of the total possible score. For example, in the chart shown, John was assigned to the Barnell Loft booklet, *Following Directions* - Level C, pages 16-22. He obtained a score of 18 out of a possible 26. Let children record their own scores if possible.

It is important that the teacher examine each child's progress. It is a misuse of materials to have the child start at page 1 or card 1 and proceed slavishly through the entire booklet or set of cards. Diagnosis of progress is the key to their effective use.

Another way to use commercial materials is to make your own individualized box. Select specific pages from various workbooks. Mount each exercise on a piece of oak tag. Number each, classify them by topic (punctuation, plurals, compound words, fractions, subtraction, map skills, magnetism, etc.) and color code them according to difficulty. Provide acetate sheets on which children can write their answers. These can be wiped clean after checking. You can make these exercises self-checking by placing the answers on the back of each card, or if that is too tempting, place answers on cards in a separate answer box.

Assign children to these exercises whenever follow-up practice is needed. If you start gradually building up this box, you will soon have an excellent individualized teaching device.

Storage

A center is generally created by a teacher to meet the specific needs or interests of particular children in the class. When a center outlives its usefulness, it should be taken down. However, this does not mean it should be destroyed. Often, a center may be adapted for different children with some slight changes. Also a center may serve as a model for other teachers. If the teacher makes notes, which may be attached to the center, of what was good and what may have been weak about the center, it will serve as a wonderful teaching device. Many of the materials made for a center were original creations and may be used again in different ways on different projects.

It is important that each teacher have a plan for the storage of completed centers. With small centers, such as those in envelopes, folders, or shoeboxes, there is little problem. They may be stored in the teacher's closet.

The difficulty comes with large centers, such as those made on posterboard or those that occupy an entire bulletin board. One effective way of storing posterboard centers is to attach them to wire coat hangers with clothespins, then hang them in a closet or on some other improvised rod just as you would a coat. When hung in this way, it is quite easy to locate any particular center.

When a center is disassembled, all the parts should be put into an envelope or box and stored in a closet. Be sure the envelope or box is clearly labeled with the name of the center, the curriculum skills or concepts involved and the dates of use.

More and more schools are setting up a central place where centers may be catalogued and checked out for use by other teachers. This is an excellent way for teachers to share ideas and reduce the work load. Often a center can't be used just as it is, but can be altered by re-writing the directions and the tasks to fit your children. If your school does not already have such arrangement, look around your building to see if there is a room or large closet that could be used for this purpose; then see if you can promote this idea among your fellow teachers. It is a good cooperative project and it removes the storage of centers from your room.

Conferences

One of the cornerstones of good learning-centered teaching is the holding of a weekly conference with each child. At this time you look through the child's folder with him to see how he is progressing and to plan for the future. Point out centers he must work in. Point out centers in which he is spending too much time. Go over errors made but be sure to praise achievement in terms of effort, creativity, conscientiousness, mastery. Find out areas of weakness, likes and dislikes.

Some teachers use the conference time to help each student make up an assignment sheet or contract form which serves as a planning guide for the coming week. A separate contract form can be made up for each subject area, or it could all be combined into one. Sample forms that one teacher used to guide her pupils in making the fullest use of the materials in her room are presented on pages 101-104.

Holding conferences is easier said than done. The problem is finding the time for them. However, the importance of having a one-to-one relationship with a child through a conference cannot be overestimated. Time snatched from other activities is easily justified. One suggestion is to use several sessions during the week when you're not doing direct teaching for conferences. Another suggestion is to meet individually with two or three children two mornings per week before school, two or three at

---

READING AND LANGUAGE ARTS ASSIGNMENT[1]

NAME _____   DATE _____

A. MATERIALS AND ASSIGNMENTS

  1. Reader: _____ Pages _____
  2. Workbook: _____ Pages _____
  3. Film Strip: Title _____ Number _____
  4. Record Player: Titles of records _____
  5. Tape Recorder: Titles _____
  6. Overhead Projector: Transparency numbers _____
  7. Centers: Numbers _____
  8. Games: _____
  9. Recreational Reading: Title _____
  10. Other: _____

B. SKILLS AND PROGRESS

  1. Writing: _____
  2. Speaking: _____
  3. Reading: _____
  4. Spelling: _____
  5. Handwriting: _____
  6. Punctuation: _____
  7. Phonics: _____
  8. Use of Dictionary: _____

---

lunch time a couple of times a week, and two or three more a couple of afternoons after school. A ten to fifteen minute session alone with the teacher might mean more to a child than three hours of doing something else.

---

1. Adapted from Perlman, Esther G., *201 Learning Center Ideas,* Bryn Mawr, Pa., I. Red Co., 1973, p. 21.

SOCIAL STUDIES ASSIGNMENT SHEET[1]

NAME _____   DATE _____

A. MATERIALS AND ASSIGNMENTS

　　1. Reference Books: Title _____ Pages _____

　　2. Film Strip: Title _____ Number _____

　　3. Projects & Activities: _____

　　4. Overhead Projector: Transparency titles _____

　　5. Centers: _____

　　6. Maps: _____

　　7. Glove: _____

　　8. Collections and Displays: _____

　　9. Flannel Board: _____

　　10. Other: _____

B. SKILLS AND PROGRESS

　　1. Current Events: _____

　　2. Famous Men: _____

　　3. Countries and Continents: _____

　　4. Government: _____

　　5. Industries: _____

　　6. Wars: _____

SCIENCE ASSIGNMENT SHEET[1]

NAME _____   DATE _____

A. MATERIALS AND ASSIGNMENTS

　　1. Books: _____ Pages _____

1. Adapted from Perlman, Esther G., *201 Learning Center Ideas*, Bryn
Mawr, Pa., I. Red Co., 1973, p. 23.

2. Nature Study Magazines: _____ Pages _____

3. Film Strip: Title _____ Number _____

4. Overhead Projector: Transparency Titles _____

5. Centers: _____

6. Games: _____

7. Experiments: _____
   Equipment Needed: Microscope _____ Scale _____
                      Stop Watch _____
                      Pliers _____ Batteries _____

8. Projects and Activities: _____
   Equipment Needed: Collections and Displays _____
                      Bulletin Board _____
                      Flannel Board _____

9. Other: _____

B. SKILLS AND PROGRESS

1. Rocks: _____

2. Magnets: _____

3. Solar System: _____

4. Plants: _____

5. Insects: _____

6. Electricity: _____

7. Air: _____

8. Weather: _____

9. Sounds: _____

10. Animals: _____

11. Space: _____

12. Birds: _____

13. Oceans: _____

14. Ecology: _____

15. Pollution: _____

MATHEMATICS ASSIGNMENT SHEET[1]

NAME _____ DATE _____

A. MATERIALS AND ASSIGNMENTS

    1. Math Box: _____ Card Nos. _____ Tape Nos. _____

    2. Film Strip: Title _____ Number _____

    3. Math Skill Builder: Title _____

    4. Flash Cards: _____

    5. Record Player: Titles _____

    6. Tape Recorder: Titles _____

    7. Centers: _____

    8. Games: _____

    9. Projects: _____
       Equipment Needed: Ruler___Yardstick___Tape Measure___
                   Scale_____Calendar_____Clock_____
                   Number Line___Place Value Chart___
                   Flannel Board_____Bulletin Board_____

  10. Other: _____

B. SKILLS AND PROGRESS

    1. Problem Solving: _____

    2. Liquid Measure: _____

    3. Money: _____

    4. Computation: _____

    5. Geometry: _____

    6. Fractions: _____

    7. Metric: _____

---

1. Adapted from Perlman, Ester G., *201 Learning Center Ideas*, Bryn
Mawr, Pa., I. Red Co., 1973, p. 22.

General Managing Suggestions

1. Have children keep a running list of books read. This
   stimulates interest in reading and can serve as the basis for
   discussing individual reading habits at conferences. A
   sample individual reading form follows. The comments
   and reactions may include plot summaries, favorite characters or events, statements of interest or lack of interest,
   statements about level of difficulty, etc.

INDIVIDUAL READING RECORD

NAME OF BOOK	DATE	TIME SPENT	PAGES READ	COMMENTS AND REACTIONS

2. One of the most important things you will have to manage is to use your own time wisely. You need time for holding conferences, circulating, asking questions, observing work habits, pin-pointing troublesome areas and identifying skills that need further practice. These teaching acts are just as critical to successful learning in your classroom as is direct teaching.

3. After all children have finished an interesting center, provide opportunities for sharing results. A discussion might do, or papers might be read or exchanged. Children derive additional learning from the center as they exchange ideas, challenge each other, ask questions, and corroborate answers.

4. Encourage children to keep a diary. This is an easy form of writing and serves as a good record of classroom occurrences.

5. In addition to centers, provide many other activities that promote oral language and vocabulary growth. These activities might include:

    Creative dramatics

    Planning a group trip

    Evaluating a trip taken

    Visit to the branch library

    Interviewing an invited guest from within or outside the school

    Conducting a poll

Reporting on research done

Ordering from a book club

Setting up a library table

Making a language bulletin board

Sending an experience story home

Listening games

Group poetry writing sessions

Role playing

Choral speaking

Conversation and discussion based on personal events, school events, current events, quotations

Storytelling

Panel discussion of current school or world issue

Classification games, such as Twenty Questions, What's My Line?

Planning class schedules

Making class rules

Oral reading by teacher or students

Listening to music

Looking at art works

Original and commercial games for thinking strategies, such as What's My Rule?, Chess, Jotto

Discussion of television programs

Book discussions

Using story films, tapes and records to stimulate discussions

6. Learning centers are a necessary and important part of a good classroom, but children need group experiences as well which help build a sense of community in the classroom. Among the projects you might consider are these:

   a. Growing flowers and vegetables.

   b. Raising animals—gerbils, hamsters, chickens, tadpoles, etc.

   c. Building scale models of the moon and planets.

   d. Social studies units—The Family, Supply and Demand, Money, The World of Yesterday, The World of Today, The World of Tomorrow, Colonial Times, Civil Rights.

   e. Science units—Dinosaurs, Space Travel, The Human Body, Electricity is Power, Magnets.

   f. Holidays—Thanksgiving, Christmas, Chanukah, Valentine's Day, Halloween, etc.

   g. Famous people—Martin Luther King, Jr., Charles Lindbergh, John F. Kennedy, Abraham Lincoln, etc.

   h. Current events—space flights, civil rights, pollution, elections, etc.

   i. Art—The Impressionists, Pop Art, etc.

   j. Cooking—cakes, popcorn, preparing for school events or parties.

   k. Music—lives of musicians, writing words for music, studying popular music.

7. Don't let the center take the place of the teacher. Children need teacher contact in small and large groups as well as on a one-to-one basis.

VII

Keeping Track

The records you keep depend upon the type of program you have and the kind of children you teach. The more individualized your program, the more records you will have to keep. The more heterogeneous your children, the greater the need for record keeping. Keep what records are necessary. You can easily get bogged down with keeping too many. A basic principle to follow is that more time should be spent on guiding and advising than on recording and marking.

But some record keeping is necessary. As has already been indicated, recording systems have to be set up so that the classroom runs smoothly and efficiently and the teacher and children know where they are supposed to be and what they are supposed to be doing. Records must also be kept to keep track of each child's progress and provide children with work that fits, interests, and challenges them.

Personal Records Kept by the Teacher

 1. *A folder for each child which might contain the following:*

    a. Check-list of skills, such as the one given in Chapter II (see pages 34-45).

    b. Contract forms

    c. Conference notes

d. Evaluation records

e. Representative samples of work

f. Scores on tests

g. Listing and scores for commercial materials used

2. *Check-list of centers completed by children.*

This may be a simple check-off sheet that shows which centers each child has completed. A sample form is shown below. Some teachers may opt to convert this form into a wall chart, in which case the children, rather than the teacher, check off their own work as they complete it.

Sample Check-list of Centers Completed

CENTER NUMBERS

NAME OF PUPIL	1	2	3	4	5	6	7	8	9	10	11	12	13	14	15
Jack A.	✔	✔		✔	✔		✔								
Sue A.	✔		✔	✔	✔	✔									
Betty B.	✔	✔													
Chip B.	✔	✔	✔												
Genie B.		✔	✔	✔	✔										
Ellen H.		✔		✔			✔		✔						
Mary L.	✔				✔		✔								
Judy M.	✔	✔	✔			✔									
Jerry M.	✔		✔	✔	✔										
Vickie O.	✔		✔	✔		✔	✔								

3. Notes on each child.

It was suggested in the previous chapter that you keep index cards handy for jotting down notes to yourself about children's progress and problems to aid you in planning new centers and small or large group sessions. Instead of, or in addition to this, you might want to keep a sheet handy that enables you to record on one page impressions about any individual child. Run off enough copies so that you have a new sheet for each day or each week.

NOTES ON INDIVIDUAL CHILDREN			Date: Nov. 19	
Jack A.	Sue A. Trouble with division	Betty B.	Chip B.	Genie B.
Ellen H.	Karen J.	Sidney K. Wrote great haiku	Mary L.	Jose L.
Carlos M. Cranky all day	Judy M.	Jerry M. Interested in snakes	Steve N. Trouble with blends	Vickie O.
Jim O.	Stephen P.	Judy P.	Ann R.	Mark R.
Sarah R.	Reba S. Started own art project	Jay S.	Alicia S.	Lenore S.
Richard T.	Aymara T.	Beth T.	Carol W.	George Z.

4. Weekly Report for Parents.

A form that goes home to parents weekly to keep them informed of the work their child is doing is a valuable adjunct to the regular report card and invaluable for parent conferences.

The children themselves can keep this record of what they do during the week and evaluate their own progress. The teacher needs only to look it over, make any necessary suggestions, and sign it before sending it home. After the parent signs it and sends it back to you, file it in each child's individual folder. A sample is shown below.

WEEKLY REPORT FOR PARENTS						
NAME _____				DATE _____		
	NAME OF CENTER	WHAT I DID	I FOLLOWED DIRECTIONS	I UNDERSTOOD WHAT I DID	I DID MY BEST	I FINISHED MY WORK
Monday						
Tuesday						
Wednesday						
Thursday						
Friday						

I need to improve in _____

TEACHER'S SIGNATURE _____ PARENT'S SIGNATURE _____

Visual Records in the Classroom

1. WALL CHARTS

Instead of a check-list sheet to show which centers each child has completed, some teachers place a wall chart in the classroom made of oaktag on which the child can check off each center as he completes it. This can be done only if an atmosphere has been established that is non-threatening to those children who don't work as fast as others, and only if it doesn't set up a competitive race which encourages children to see who can finish the most centers first.

This chart can be exactly like the check-list described before (see page 111). Instead of putting a check or an X in a box to indicate a completed center, have children color in the block with magic markers. If each child selects a different color each time he colors in a block, you will end up with an esthetically appealing chart that looks somewhat like a Mondrian painting.

Another way to use the wall chart is to add a check-off system for the teacher. The box for each center is divided into half. The child puts the date he finished a center in the upper half of the box, and the teacher enters the date he checked and approved the work done in the lower half. This shows the teacher at a glance which work he has to look over and tends to provide children with the needed teacher feedback more quickly. See sample wall chart on opposite page.

2. CHECK SHEETS AT CENTERS

Another alternative for visual recording is to place a check-list of all the children's names at each center. Each child checks off his name as he finishes the center. This approach is less public than the wall chart. It also gives children who have worked at the same center a chance to chat about their work. And it has the advantage that it quickly shows the teacher when a center has exhausted its usefulness and needs to be taken down.

A record of completed centers must be kept in order that the teacher may know something about the popularity of each

Sample Wall Chart of Centers Completed

CENTERS

NAME	1	2	3	4	5	6	7	8	9	10
Jack A.	2/3 2/4	2/3 2/4	2/7	2/4 2/4	2/5 2/7					
Sue A.	2/3 2/4	2/7	2/3 2/4	2/5 2/7	2/6 2/7					
Betty B.										
Chip B.										
Genie B.										

center, and about the activity of each child. The teacher may choose to keep these records in his personal files, or he may prefer a visual system that informs and involves the children. It will probably depend on what kind of class he has.

One other advantage of a visual system is that if a teacher wants to institute peer tutoring on some scale, posting a chart enables a child who may have some question or problem while working at a center to consult with one of the children who have completed the work at that center.

Evaluation

Evaluation must be done regularly, continuously, and consistently. Several different types of evaluation need to be planned.

1. OVERALL EVALUATION

Formal measuring instruments such as standarized tests, and informal instruments such as inventories, check-lists, teacher-made tests, in-book tests, criterion referenced tests, and teacher observation and judgment are necessary regardless of what form the teaching takes. It is important to have written records that show what children have been doing, and how well they have been doing. Evaluation systems have a particularly important place in learning-centered teaching in order to assess results of the program, as well as for planning and re-planning the content of the program. In an individualized program which offers children educational choices, means must be provided for keeping track of each child's progress.

2. PRODUCT EVALUATION

Overall evaluation generally shows academic achievement and progress in skills. The individual finished products of children also have to be evaluated. However, if the teacher undertakes the marking of every paper done, he will scarcely have time for anything else. Various approaches might be taken that are equally effective in providing feedback to children.

Whenever possible, each center should be self-checking. It is good for children to take responsibility for the quality of their own work. It is good for them to regard the teacher as someone who helps with problems and questions, and not just as someone who checks or approves. Checking and approving of and for oneself builds confidence, independence and intrinsic motivation.

There are children who will cheat when given this right, but my experience has been that the amount of cheating reduces itself the more self-checking children are permitted to do. Perhaps they come to realize that when they cheat, they are only cheating themselves—a very important lesson to learn.

Spot-check work in centers that are not self-checking. Generally, this kind of work does not have right or wrong answers and does not earn specific scores. It is important that this work be encouraged by getting appropriate attention. There are other means besides teacher approval for doing this. Peer approval is very important. Displaying work on bulletin boards, exchanging work with classmates, submitting work for publication in school newspapers are all excellent sources of feedback.

You may also have children keep their finished products in

their folders, and look through them to check and evaluate the quality of the work during individual conferences.

3. SELF-EVALUATION

Learning particular skills and facts is not the only growth expected from learning centers. Children should also be acquiring better study habits, self-direction, self-discipline, and responsibility. Help children to develop criteria for evaluating their own progress in centers. These criteria might be posted on a chart. A typical one might look like this:

How We Work in Centers

1. We arrange for the materials we will need.

2. We use our time wisely.

3. We proofread our work.

4. We finish each job we start. If we don't finish, why?

5. We put our finished work in the correct place.

6. We put things away.

7. We leave the center ready for the next person to use.

Each week have a group evaluation session. Discuss the criteria on the chart to see what progress is taking place. Revise the chart if necessary. You might also discuss such matters as what centers need changing, what new materials are needed, whether or not learning is taking place, what is interfering with or helping learning take place.

A further means of self-evaluation is through an evaluation form that each child fills in weekly. Children place them in their

SELF-EVALUATION SHEET[1]

NAME _____ DATE _____

1. I finished these centers this week _____

2. This week I enjoyed working in the _____ Center best.

3. I was able to do most of the work in the centers.

　　　　　　YES　　　　NO

4. I remembered to put my name and date on all my papers.

　　　　　　YES　　　　NO

5. I used good manners while in the Learning Centers.

　　　　　　YES　　　　NO

6. I put all my finished papers where they belong.

　　　　　　YES　　　　NO

7. I had trouble working in these centers.

　　　　　　YES　　　　NO

　　because _____

8. I need help with _____

9. I need more practice in _____

10. I am improving in _____

11. I would rate my work this week:
　　Excellent　　Good　　Average　　Fair　　Poor

12. I tried to help my classmates this week.

　　　　　　YES　　　　NO

13. I think we could improve our centers if we _____

_____　　　　_____
Student's Signature　　　　*Teacher's Signature*

folders to be discussed at the weekly conference. Other samples of evaluation forms can be found in the Appendix.

Involving Children in Record Keeping

Except for the notes and forms kept by the teacher in his own file, most of the forms and records suggested here should be clearly explained to and understood by the children. Whenever possible, children should be directly involved in creating the recording form and in keeping it up to date. This not only teaches children good organizational skills, but makes them aware and responsible for their own educational progress.

It has already been suggested that each child maintain a folder. This may be the same folder used by the teacher, or a separate one. There should be a designated place (file or carton or box) where these folders are kept. The folders may contain: skill check-lists, centers completed, contract forms, self-evaluation forms, list of books read, completed work to be checked, diary, and such.

Keep your record-keeping system as simple as possible. If you don't, it could end up with the tail wagging the dog. A number of systems have been suggested. Sift through them to find those which best suit you, or create others that are more satisfactory. A number of other possible record keeping forms appear in the Appendix.

1. Adapted from Perlman, Esther G., *201 Learning Center Ideas*, Bryn Mawr, Pa., I. Red Co., 1973, p. 27.

VIII

Administrative Support

A school is a cooperative enterprise, not simply a number of teachers each practicing his lonely craft in his own room in the same building. Regardless of the qualifications of individual members of a school staff, the quality of the total program depends on how well the staff works together in producing a good educational program for the community. Teachers should be related to each other by the philosophy of the school, by the plan of the curriculum, by sharing ideas, by their mutual concern for the children. Teachers need and deserve supervision, assistance, and support, as well as individual recognition and identification with the total enterprise.

These things don't just happen. They must be guaranteed by the way in which the school is organized. This is the chief function of a school principal. The right leadership given by the principal is the only real answer for bringing about a feeling of community among teachers. The principal is the greatest determinant of the character of the school.

The level of teacher performance is an essential responsibility of the principal. It is he who can do something about teacher performance. He largely has control of the selection process; he can improve the curriculum planning process; he can provide the means for continuous professional development through in-service activities; and he can provide as good a working climate for teaching as is possible. Teachers alone can do little about the quality of education; principals and teachers working together can do a lot.

Providing Leadership

The principal is primarily responsible for introducing innovative changes into a school program. He must be in touch with the most current research findings and choose the most promising methods and approaches. Since he sets the atmosphere and philosophy of the school, he must select carefully those new trends that are consistent with his conceived educational goals, and he must educate his staff to the purposes and methodologies of any new approach.

For learning-centered education to operate successfully in a school, there has to be solid agreement between teachers and principal on their purpose and desirability. There are many things the principal can do to bring this about. Some suggestions follow.

1. Learn all you can about learning centers. Attend workshops, read books, visit other schools where you can observe the program in action, and discuss it with these teachers and other educators. Start a center program in your own school only after you have become convinced that centers will bring about the type of individualization and learning climate that you believe will improve your school.

2. The institution of a learning-centered program should be a democratic process. The initial idea for starting centers might come from either teachers or you. If it doesn't come from teachers, and you are convinced it is the direction you would like your school to take, then it is your responsibility and right to suggest it. But you can't mandate it. Teachers may not be ready.

Provide a period of preparation through an in-service program. Encourage teachers to read books. Arrange for them to visit classrooms where they can observe centers in use. Invite persons to give demonstrations, conduct workshops, and lead discussions. Help teachers learn as much about it as they can. Help them to become as enthusiastic and knowledgeable as you are. Don't do all the telling. Wait until they are ready to embrace learning-centered teaching on their own.

3. Help the faculty commit their goals and objectives to writing. There is a better chance of achieving what you want if explicit goals are set. Use operational terms; the more explicit the better it can be implemented and evaluated. For example, "By November 1, all teachers will have at least one learning center in their classroom." "Learning centers will promote more individualization, as evidenced by the variability of tasks engaged in by children at a given session."

4. Monitor the development of the program in terms of the goals set with the teachers. If they know what to expect, they will regard monitoring as helpful rather than as threatening. Aspects which need to be monitored: are centers based on assessment, are centers used to individualize, format of the center, quality of materials and content, frequency of change, record keeping, and room organization.

5. Use positive reinforcement. Whenever you observe a worthwhile practice, acknowledge it and mention it at a faculty meeting. Teachers are motivated when their efforts are appreciated.

6. Hold faculty meetings in different classrooms. This acquaints teachers with each other's work. It also gives each

teacher the opportunity to explain his or her program and to get feedback from colleagues. Occasionally, instead of a formal faculty meeting, spend the time having the group tour different classrooms.

7. Move slowly, allowing each teacher to proceed at his own pace. Give them the freedom to select their model (see Chapter 4), but encourage them to move on to more refined models. Respect the fact that, just as with any other approach, not all teachers can be equally good at center teaching. Individual differences among teachers must be respected in the same way as we do for children. If you are patient about the difficulties involved in running a learning-centered classroom, teachers will be more motivated to overcome the difficulties, realizing the importance of improving the way we teach children to live in a more open society.

8. Take into consideration the extra time needed for preparing learning centers, for continuous planning, and for evaluation and refinement of the program. Allow teachers some time to work on centers during the school day along with fellow teachers. Early dismissal twice per month, using in-service days, setting up a schedule so that each teacher has a daily free period, freeing teachers to work together by scheduling several classes for art, music, gym at the same time will pay dividends in an improved program, as well as in good will.

9. Set up a teacher center where teachers can go to prepare centers. Stock it with consumable supplies and with needed equipment such as paper cutters, a laminating machine, scraps, junk. Books from which they may obtain ideas should also be provided.

10. Find space to set up a lending library of centers that were

prepared and used by teachers. This library also helps teachers with the storage problem after their children have finished using a center.

11. Encourage special teachers of art, music, and physical education to utilize the center approach in their areas. They might place centers they have arranged in their own rooms or in regular classrooms. When the approach by all the teachers in a school is consistent, the children benefit.

12. It is important to budget money for consumable supplies. Ample availability of these materials indicates to teachers the support of the administration.

13. Develop a research design to evaluate whether learning centers produce better educational results. Include instruments that attempt to measure both congnitive and affective growth. Teachers should be involved in developing the design and in interpreting the results.

14. Make every effort to keep the community involved and informed about your new educational program.

Teachers Who Don't Want to Change

Among any group of teachers there are likely to be some who don't want to change from their former approaches. This may be because of uncertainty, insecurity, rigidity, or lack of conviction. To make the program go, all these problems have to be faced.

One stop-gap you have is that some children, because of learning disabilities, personality, physical conditions, may not be suited to a learning-centered classroom. It overwhelms them to the extent that they cannot learn as well, and their presence in these busy rooms impedes the progress of other children. Some parents, despite your efforts to inform them, will refuse to have their children participate in a learning-centered classroom because it appears too unstructured or too undisciplined. For these reasons you often need to retain some traditional classrooms, perhaps one at each grade level. These classes can take care of teachers who find change difficult.

Those teachers who have been successful all along, but face change with uncertainty and reluctance need to be reassured that they have your enthusiastic support, that you will not let them fail. Ask them to start with a simple model. Give them all the help and encouragement you can. My experience has been that teachers who overcome their fears enough to try learning centers, get involved with them and do not want to go back to their former methods.

Occasionally, you may have a teacher who jumps enthusiastically at the opportunity to try something different, but then finds the effort to change overwhelming. Give them time. Let them stay with the simplest model as long as they need to. Some of these teachers make a slow start and then begin to blossom.

The teacher who is unwilling to change and cannot accept the learning-centered philosophy may respond to direct and logical appeal by colleagues to attempt it on a very small scale. Few people like to feel like outsiders. While no teacher's job should be threatened by any curriculum decision, everyone who holds a teaching position owes it to the organization to support the prevailing philosophy. Ultimately, a teacher who is uncomfortable with the new approach, and uncomfortable being the lone hold-out, may voluntarily remove himself to another school where he will fit better into the program.

Educating Parents

Parents may become severe critics of any change within a school unless they are involved in the planning and understand the change. It is the principal who must take the leadership in promoting the learning-centered approach among parents.

Involve parents from the beginning. Through newsletters, public meetings, or meetings with small groups, help them understand why the learning-centered classroom is desirable. They may welcome a departure from the factory model of education that stressed conformity of behavior and method and failed to meet their children's needs. They can understand that schools, like other institutions such as banks, factories, medicine, and law, must continually change in order to keep abreast of changes in society.

Let them know the extensive preparation teachers are receiving. Explain your time-line and the research design.

Arrange demonstrations for them. Encourage them to visit classrooms to see first-hand what the program is. Put on adult-oriented workshops in which the parents perform tasks in centers. Discuss the results with them. Make the professional library on learning centers available to them. Encourage them to read and discuss the approach.

An informed community is one of the greatest allies of schools. Don't overlook this important aspect of giving leadership to learning-centered education.

IX

Informing Parents

To parents, the term "learning centers" is nebulous and as mysterious as a foreign language. Parents are concerned about the education of their children. They deserve to know everything about it that they want to know. It is up to the principal to inform and educate parents and gain their support for the new program. But it is up to teachers to keep parents knowledgeable and enthusiastic about the ongoing activities and results of learning-centered teaching.

Techniques for Informing Parents

Some teachers prefer written contacts, others would rather have in-person presentations. Each teacher should choose those approaches which best fit his own style and beliefs, but some communication must take place to prevent a gap between teacher and parents. Among the suggestions which follow there will be something to fit each temperament.

PICTURE OR SLIDE PRESENTATION

The teacher may call a meeting of parents at which he will show pictures or slides of centers and children at work in them. This gives him an opportunity to explain his organization and the reasons for centers. Using pictures of the actual children makes for increased interest and is less abstract and more personal than a lecture or discussion.

CLASSROOM VISITS

Invite parents to visit the classroom during center time in order to see at first-hand how the program works. You might give each parent a specific job, such as supervising Center 8, to make them feel more at ease. Ask them to visit each center to observe children at work and to study the content of the center. Some teachers assign a pupil to each parent to serve as a guide in learning about the setup.

To make the visits most effective, send each parent a note inviting him to visit on a specific date and time. Arrange your time so that you are available to talk with them. If possible, arrange a discussion session immediately following their visit.

DISCUSSIONS WITH SMALL GROUPS

Invite two or three parents at a time to come during lunch hour or after school to discuss your center approach. Show them around the room. Give them a chance to ask questions. Get their reactions to their children's working in centers.

ENLISTING VOLUNTEERS

Invite parents to volunteer to come to help in your room during center time. Give them specific tasks, such as supervising certain centers, answering children's questions, marking papers, helping make new centers, and such. Involving parents directly not only helps them gain a good understanding of centers, but gives you and the children needed extra hands. If you could recruit ten volunteers, each to come at a different time, not only would you be helping these ten parents and the others they would be telling about it, but your program would be considerably enhanced. Be sure to obtain a commitment from each parent to serve at a specific time, except in emergencies.

SENDING CHILDREN'S WORK HOME

If you ask a child what he did in school, the typical response is "Nothing." Most children are not very good at volunteering information, even when asked. Most parents welcome concrete evidence of what their children are doing in school.

It was suggested in Chapter VII *(see page 113)* that children complete a form about their work in centers that goes home each week for parents to examine and sign. Other forms appear in the Appendix.

In addition, after the teacher has checked children's work it may go home.

READINGS

You might build up a classroom library, or get your school to do so, of books about centers. Books might be selected from the Bibliography at the end of this book. Also accumulate magazine or journal articles as they appear. Make the books and articles available for parents to read. You might from time to time send home a brief Parents Newsletter with short reviews of current material that may interest parents, and tell them how they may avail themselves of these. If there is enough interest, you might occasionally hold a book seminar after school.

WRITTEN COMMUNICATIONS

By means of newletters or explanatory papers, inform parents about your program and about new centers. Invite parental feedback.

You might prepare a short handbook that explains concisely the essentials of learning centers. Descriptions of centers might be included. The following statements are excerpted from such handbooks.

> Learning centers are established in the classroom to
> provide opportunities to meet your child's needs and
> interests. Centers are made to reinforce and enrich
> various skills and concepts already taught in class. They

offer a comfortable means for those children who are ready to move on in various areas. They also help those children who need extra help and reinforcement.

Through samples of your child's daily work, I want to communicate to you how well your child is progressing. At least every other week I will have a conference with your child concerning his work at centers. At these conferences I hope to gain a greater insight into your child's progress and needs. We will go over center worksheets together to discuss problems or answer questions.

After we have these conferences I will send home the papers. There will be one paper with your child's signature and mine. I would like for you to examine your child's papers, then sign the form, and send it back to me. I hope this will help you learn more about your child's progress and achievement.[1]

Another teacher wrote in her handbook:

Learning in Centerville!

I am very happy to have your child in my classroom this year. Your child will be involved in a learning-centered classroom, along with regular small group instruction.

This type of classroom will, I believe, motivate each child and help him or her learn skills in a unique way. I strongly feel that the learning-centered classroom will provide your child with a very human and individualized learning experience.

A learning-centered classroom is used for introducing and reinforcing concepts and skills, as well as for developing interests. Various activities will be assigned

---

1. Prepared by Patricia DeCostanza, Edgewood Elementary School, Ridley School District, Folsom, Pa.

to, or chosen by, the child each week. Each child will fill
in a contract to show what he or she plans to accomplish
each week.

Each child will also have an individual conference
with me each week concerning his or her work. All of
my comments will be placed in each child's folder to be
read any time by you or the child.

Hopefully you have seen some of our centers. If you
can, come and visit my classroom this year to see the
children working.[1]

A complete handbook prepared by a third grade teacher is
included in the Appendix. In it the teacher explains her program
for the year and shows clearly how learning centers are
integrated into the school day. Concrete examples are included.

WORKSHOPS

One of the most effective means for informing parents is by
conducting a workshop in which they actually work in centers.
This gives them a direct experience of what centers are and how
their children feel about working in them. If your PTA conducts
a Back-to-School Night, a workshop might be your most
effective way to familiarize your parents with your program,
particularly your centers. Two workshops are described here.

Sample Workshop I[2]

1. When all the parents are assembled in a group, role play a
   traditional classroom with a very strict and formal at-

---

1. Prepared by Sharon Guarente, Sharon Hill Elementary School,
   Southeast Delco School District, Sharon Hill, Pa.

2. Many of these ideas were suggested by Pat DiCostanza, Pat
   Douglass, John Harmes, Diane Lambert, Maxine Segal, and Sima
   Wolf.

mosphere—straight rows, no talking, no questions. As the teacher, you do all the talking. Give simple commands—fold your hands, two feet on the floor, etc.

Teach a ten minute lesson on a subject appropriate to your grade level. Call on "students" for answers. Insist on full, correct responses. Reprimand those who do not follow the rules.

2. When the formal lesson is over, assign parents to work in several centers which you have set up. Give them directions, and tell them that when they have finished you will have a discussion with them. Set a deadline for finishing. Some of the centers you might set up are:

● *Name Tags* Place all sorts of materials and supplies on a table. Mount a set of directions telling parents to construct name tags. They may be any size, shape, color, composition the parent wants, but they must include the same basic information—name of parent, name of child, how many other siblings, address.

● *Let's Find Out* Place pencils and three sets of cards on a table. One set is headed: Things I Would Like You to Know About Me. Another set is headed: Things I Would Like You to Know About My Child. A third set is headed: Things I Would Like to Know About You. In your set of instructions, tell parents they may write as little or as much as they like, and that they may indicate which information may be shared with the other parents. Indicate that you would like to be able to call on them to participate in various class activities and are especially interested in their jobs, interests, hobbies, talents and skills.

● *Feelings* Place magic markers or crayons near a

blank mural. In your instructions ask parents to make a design on part of the mural that expresses how they feel about their evening at school. Discuss this mural at the sit-down discussion session.

● *Bad News! Good News!* Provide the various forms that you regularly need parents to fill out, such as milk orders, book clubs, field trip slips, etc. Give instructions for filling them out and for where to put them when completed.

● *Where Are We Going?* On a desk have ditto sheets or a booklet or handbook with your objectives for the year. Instruct parents to read this. Provide paper and ask them to write their questions and comments. Suggest that they list any objectives you have not included that they would like to see.

● *Help!* Have a sign-up sheet asking parents to sign up for voluntary time to assist you in the classroom. Have other forms on which they may indicate when they would like to come to visit school.

● *Fill-Up* Have a snack center with coffee, tea, cookies. Instruct parents to help themselves, to introduce themselves to other parents in this center, and to chat about their experiences of the evening.

● *Seeing Is Believing* Set up an automatic carousel slide projector, or have an album of snapshots of the children actually at work at centers. Try to include every child in the class. Have paper available on which parents can jot down their reactions to the pictures.

● *For Men Only!* Assign fathers only to work at this center. Set up a totally "female type" activity such as embroidery, sewing a button, mending a rip, or such.

Have instructions and reaction sheets available.

• *For Women Only!* Assign mothers only to work at this center. Set up a "masculine type" activity such as hammering or using a screw driver or wrench, changing a light switch, wiring a battery circuit. Have instructions and reaction sheets available.

• *Junk* Provide materials such as tin cans, plastic containers, mixing bowls, measuring cups and spoons, raw noodles of all kinds, lumber odds and ends, screws, nails, tools, bottle caps, styrofoam, egg cartons, needles, thread, spools, buttons, aluminum, yarn, TV dinner trays, scraps of fabric. Have several instruction sheets for parents to choose from: some suggesting math measuring and counting activities and exercises; some suggesting art activities creating collages and sculptures. Have mimeographed lists of these materials and ask parents to take the lists home and send in any of these supplies with their children.

3. After everyone has finished, hold a discussion and have parents share their feelings about the two forms of teaching and discuss any questions they might have. Use this time to get across any ideas or information you might want to convey.

Sample Workshop II[1]

In this workshop, after the parents assemble, they are given an instruction sheet which explains that they are going to work in centers and instructs them in what to do. A sample instruction sheet follows.

---

1. Developed by Elaine Powell, Lois Lury, and Kathy Riehs, Hillcrest Elementary School, Upper Darby, Pa.

Instruction Sheet

Good evening! Welcome to our Open House Workshop! This evening you will be "walking in your child's footsteps" by participating in a learning-centered classroom. Your child's center time each day is designed in a similar manner.

Here's what to do: Complete the work at each of the 8 centers which you will find on the tables around the room. If more than 3 persons are at a center (except for number 8) when you go there, go to another one. You'll find directions at each center. Check off each center on your list as you complete it. Finish all centers by 9:00 P.M.; then we'll all sit down and discuss what you've done and what your children do.

CENTER CHECK-LIST

1. Family portraits   _____

2. Flashcards   _____

3. Volunteer!   _____

4. Workbooks   _____

5. Storybooks   _____

6. Figure It Out!   _____

7. Questionnaire   _____

8. Opinions (Do this last)   _____

---

1. *Family Portraits* Have drawing paper, magic markers, flair pens, large sheets of construction paper, glue, and a snapshot of each child in the class available at this center. Each parent

draws his own self-portrait. Parents also draw pictures of their other children. They then mount these portraits and the snapshot of their child to a sheet of construction paper, decorate it in any way they like, and label it, "The _____ Family." They hang their product on a clothesline in the room.

2. *Flashcards* Make a number of flashcards on which you write phrases such as: Builds self-reliance. Is teacher-centered. Is noisy. Has no structure. Builds independence. Emphasizes basic education. Is frustrating for children. Lets children do whatever they want., etc. Have a ditto sheet with two columns headed True and Untrue. Direct parents to write each phrase on the ditto sheet in the column where they think it belongs in relation to the learning-centered classroom. Encourage them to discuss the phrases freely with other parents who might be at this center at the same time. Have a folder where they can put their sheets, and discuss them later on when all the centers have been finished.

3. *Volunteer!* Ask parents to sign up for the various kinds of volunteer help needed in the classroom. For example, field trips, class parties, making materials, supervising centers, tutoring in reading, reading to children, sharing hobbies and interests, etc. Have a ditto sheet on which they can indicate what they would like to do and when.

4. *Workbooks* Have copies of various workbooks the children use for reinforcement and for individualization in different subject areas. Direct parents to examine the workbooks, select a page at random and do the work on a separate piece of paper. Discuss the place and purpose of workbooks in the curriculum at the subsequent discussion.

5. *Storybooks* Have available a number of representative read-

ing materials used by the children. Provide a ditto sheet with headings classifying the books by categories, such as: fiction, history, biography, autobiography, poetry, science fiction, reference. Direct the parents to skim some of the books and write their titles under the correct classification category on the sheet. This center allows you to explain during the discussion period your independent reading program, and to suggest ways that parents might be of assistance.

6. *Figure It Out!* Mount a picture of some common object, such as a soft drink bottle, a sweater, a shoe, a brick, or such, to a piece of oaktag. Cut a piece of construction paper to the same size as the oaktag. Put a number in the upper right-hand corner. Cut one or two small holes in the construction paper. Attach it to the oaktag by sealing the edges. Through the holes, parts of the object can be seen. Ask the parents to use their best observational and deductive powers to try to figure out what the object is. Have them record on a sheet of paper at the center their name and what they think the object is.

Have magazines, oaktag, construction paper, scissors, tape, available at the center. Instruct parents to make a Figure It Out puzzle of their own, number it, and leave it at the center for other parents to try to guess. Later on, during the discussion, reveal the pictures and have parents discuss their reactions to this experience.

7. *Questionnaire* On a sheet of paper list a number of controversial topics which frequently create a generation gap, such as: allowances, curfews, R-rated movies, TV, homework, teenage marriage. Ask parents to choose a topic that interests them and complete a questionnaire on this topic.

Your questionnaires should list between five and ten questions for each topic. Try to use the Yes-No format. Avoid very personal questions, but do try to explore the attitudes of the parents compared to the attitudes of their children.

During the discussion period, parents will enjoy sharing their views and problems with each other.

8. *Opinions* Have ditto sheets on which parents can respond to the following questions:

How does tonight's experience differ from the experience you had when you went to school?

How do you think your child feels about his learning center activities?

Do you feel you have a better understanding of learning centers? List at least three ideas you got tonight as the result of working in centers.

Please write down any questions, comments or ideas you might have that we can discuss as a group later tonight.

Are you glad you came?

Conclusion

There are many different ways to educate children, ranging from the most traditional subject-matter oriented institutions to the most radical child-centered schools which even give children a choice of whether or not they want to attend class at all. The particular curriculum design adopted by any school and staff reflects their philosophy of education, what they consider the goals of education to be, and their concept of what constitute optimum learning conditions.

In this book, the learning-centered approach has been described in detail and its philosophical bases presented. The learning-centered classroom seeks to build a humanistic environment for children in which they can thrive emotionally and socially, while concurrently learning needed academic skills and basic knowledge. For this educational approach to succeed requires the enthusiastic understanding and cooperative efforts of teachers, administrators and parents.

It is the hope of the author that people who are attracted to this philosophy and approach, but who are hesitant about actually trying it for fear they don't know how, will take courage from this book.

X

Sample Learning Centers

In this chapter are presented some representative learning centers. Each one is complete and may be used by any teacher who may find it appropriate for his particular class. However, the intention is not to present the teacher with a blueprint, but rather with a prototype so that he may have a very clear idea of how to go about creating similar materials designed specifically for his students.

These learning centers cover selected topics in the language arts, math, science and social studies. Material is presented at a range of grade levels. Some of the centers are designed for initial teaching, some for reinforcement; some centers focus on skill building, some on broad concept development; some centers are designed for use by the entire class, some for selected students.

It will be observed that regardless of subject and grade level, certain features are common to all the learning centers. We have divided each presentation into two parts, the first part being for the student, and the second part for the teacher.

The picture of the learning center is exactly what the student sees. It is self-contained, in the sense that it includes everything the student will need to work at the center. Each center has some graphic device to depict its subject and to engage the student's interest. Attached to each learning center is an envelope or pocket labeled *Objective, Materials, Directions, Evaluation, On*

Your Own. In the envelope or pocket are sheets with the designated information. We believe that every student should know what the objective of the learning center is. Giving each student his own list of materials needed and directions not only makes it possible for students to function independently with minimal help from the teacher, but also presents the student with a model of orderliness and organization that he may well emulate.

Each learning center includes some means whereby the student can evaluate his own work. In some cases, where questions are primarily objective, answer sheets are provided. Where tasks are more subjective, ways have been suggested for students to receive feedback on their work. In either case, it is felt that an immediate response is important. When students are working alone, it is necessary to build in opportunities for interaction.

Each center also contains suggestions for additional independent work for students. Obviously, some students will be interested in doing more, and some will not be. All their efforts, whether slight or extensive, should be acknowledged and approved.

The section for the teacher includes an explanation of the *Objective, Directions* for making the center, and a *Discussion* with additional teaching suggestions. The difference between the statement of objectives for the student and for the teacher is that the student is told what he can expect to do and achieve at this center; the teacher is told where in the scheme of academic goals this particular center's activity fits.

Complete and specific directions are given the teacher for making the center. The directions describe the particular center presented here; the teacher is, of course, encouraged to make innovations on his own freely.

The discussion section may list skills or experiences that would be required before students could be expected to use the learning center. Or it might describe variations for the activity, or present suggestions for further preparation or for follow-up.

Getting Acquainted

LEARNING CENTER NO. 1   ALL SUBJECTS   ALL LEVELS

*Developed from ideas contributed by Betty van Arsdale.

SPINNER WELCOMES YOU TO SCHOOL

For the Student

Objectives

You will do ten different activities. These will help you to become familiar with learning stations or centers and with your classmates and teacher.

Materials

You will need a pen or pencil and magic markers. Any other materials you may need will be available at the centers.

Directions

1. Take an Instruction Sheet from the envelope.
2. Find the station number that is starred. Do this station first. You will find additional directions at each center.
3. Follow in numerical order until you have completed station number 10. Then go back to station number 1 and continue until you have done all ten stations.
4. Check off each station on your Instruction Sheet as you complete each one.

Evaluation

Most of the centers need no checking, or are self-checking, but we would like you to evaluate the learning center approach.

When you have completed all the stations, on the back of your instruction sheet write your opinion of this way of getting acquainted on the first day of school.

Also, tell which center you enjoyed most and which center you enjoyed least.

Place your paper in the Opinions envelope at the center.

On Your Own

1. As you go around the room working at the various centers, chat with your classmates. Exchange ideas and views about

school in general, and about the learning centers in particular.

2. Do you have any suggestions for other learning centers that could be used on the first day of school? Write your ideas on a sheet of paper and put it in the Opinions envelope.

Suggestions for the Teacher—Learning Center No. 1

Objectives

The opening day of school is an exciting and anxious time for children. Often it is an overpowering experience with everything teacher-centered in a rather regimented fashion. Using a learning-centered plan can serve several purposes. This approach gives the child a short, rather stimulating introduction to learning centers. It also allows the teacher to mingle with and observe children in a way that is not possible in a more traditional approach. Children and teacher begin to get to know each other in a relaxed, informal way that builds trust and confidence.

Basic information that the teacher needs from each child can be gathered at various stations. Also, the teacher can begin to get some idea of each child's academic skills, which will help in the construction of the first few centers for the new school year.

Directions for Making the Center

1. Place this center on a very conspicuous bulletin board. Use colored construction paper or posterboard to make your cartoon character. You might use a made-up character, such as Spinner, or you might use well-known characters, such as Snoopy or Charlie Brown, or a TV personality, such as Kotter or the Fonz.

Arrange circle cut-outs of different colors, with numbers on them, in game-board fashion on the center to indicate the ten station points. Use narrow strips of colored construction paper to make a path between each station.

2. Mount envelopes on the bulletin board for the general directions, Instruction and Opinion Sheets. Run off enough

SPINNER WELCOMES YOU TO SCHOOL

Instruction Sheet

Today you will work at 10 different learning stations around the classroom.

Start with the station number that is starred and move from one station to the next in numerical order, going back to number one when you complete number 10. Be sure you complete all the stations. Check each station off on this sheet as you finish it.

After you complete all the stations, turn this paper over and on the back write your opinion of this way of spending the first day at school.

Have fun!

Ready? Go!

Stations

1. Names and Faces   _____

2. Background Basics   _____

3. Feelings   _____

4. Who's in Class?   _____

5. Helping Hands   _____

6. Stock Up   _____

7. Handwriting Analysis   _____

8. Spin a Tale   _____

9. Dice-a-Mathics   _____

10. Spellbound   _____

_____   _____

Name   *Date*

Instruction Sheets so that each student has one. Star one of the numbers on each sheet to indicate where the student is to begin. This will limit the number of students at a center to three or four.

3. Make the 10 Spinner stations on sheets of colored oaktag. Draw your cartoon character in a different pose at the top of each center. Print the instructions for each center on the oaktag. Laminate the oaktag or cover it with clear contact paper.

4. Place the stations on tables, bulletin boards, or desks scattered as widely around the room as possible in order to allow for free movement. Be sure that all needed materials are available at each station.

5. You may use the following stations as samples:

STATION 1   **Names and Faces**

1. Take a name tag and write your name on it with the magic marker. Attach it to your blouse or shirt.

2. Check your name on the attendance list posted at this station.

3. Take a piece of drawing paper and draw a portrait of yourself using the crayons. Hang your finished portrait on the clothesline by the window.

STATION 2   **Background Basics**

1. Take a questionnaire from the envelope. Fill out all the information carefully.

2. Place your completed paper in the basket.

NOTE TO TEACHER: Your questionnaire may cover such data as: name, nickname, birthdate, address, phone number, father's and mother's names and places of employment, names of brothers and sisters, subjects most liked and disliked, hobbies, best friend's name, etc.

STATION 3   **Feelings**

1. How do you feel today? Are you: excited? nervous? happy? busy? lazy?

2. You know that colors can suggest moods. For example, bright colors look happy, dark colors look serious. Designs can suggest moods too—curves and circles suggest different things than lines and angles.

3. The mural paper at this station has been divided into squares. There is one square for each student. Select one of the blocks as your own. Using the magic markers, draw a design (not a picture) that expresses how you feel about this, the first day of school.

STATION 4   **Who's in Class?**

1. Take a work sheet from the envelope. It has the names of everyone in the class written in a scrambled fashion.

2. Try to unscramble your classmates' names. Write your answers next to each scramble.

3. When you've finished, check your answers with the attendance list at Station 1. Correct any errors you may have made.

4. Keep your finished list for your own use.

5. Try to get to know everyone's name and face. On a sheet of paper, try to list as many names as you can remember without looking at your list. Did you remember most of them?

6. Go and look at the clothesline where students have hung their self-portraits. See if you can match the names with the pictures.

STATION 5   **Helping Hands**

1. Look at the job list posted at this station.

2. Read the job requirements for each.

3. Sign up for any one job. We will rotate the jobs later on so that everyone has as many different jobs as possible during the year.

NOTE TO TEACHER: Include such jobs as leader, lunch count, trash, chalkboards, messenger, etc.

STATION 6   **Stock Up**

1. In the envelope you will find a copy of the list of school supplies we will need this year.

2. Read it carefully. Check the items you already have. Put an X beside those you don't think you have.

3. Take the list home and show it to your parents. See if they can help you fill in any of the supplies you are missing. Have them sign the list.

4. Return the list to me tomorrow.

5. Bring in all the supplies you checked on your list.

NOTE TO TEACHER: Include on the list the supplies each child will need (pencils, notebook, etc.) and also supplies the class may need later on (jars, plastic spoons, containers, etc.)

STATION 7   **Handwriting Analysis**

1. Handwriting analysts tell a lot about people's personalities from the way they write—from the size and shape of their letters, the slant and spacing. You will rate your own handwriting.

2. Take a Handwriting Analysis sheet from the envelope. Copy the typewritten sentence at the top of the

page on the blank lines. Using this as your handwriting sample, rate yourself for each item on the form. Be as honest as you can.

3. Put your completed form into the basket.

NOTE TO TEACHER: The Handwriting Analysis form should require children to evaluate their speed, legibility, neatness, impulsivity, etc. Provide a rating scale for each item so children can check the answer they think is most appropriate, e.g. My writing is usually ☐very large ☐large ☐medium ☐small ☐tiny.

STATION 8   **Spin a Tale**

Spinner had a wonderful summer. His master had been at home with him, and each day Marco and Spinner found some exciting thing to do.

But now the summer was over. Today Marco went off on his first "back to school" day. Spinner was all alone. He thought about some of the lovely things they had done that summer. He wondered what he should do now.

Then he fell asleep.

1. Take a sheet of paper from the pile and write a paragraph or two about Spinner's dream.

2. Give your story a title.

3. At the bottom of your story, tell whether you want the teacher to read it to himself or to the rest of the class.

4. Put your paper in the basket.

STATION 9   **Dice-a-Mathics**

1. This is a simple game of chance. You don't need skill, but you do need to know how to add and multiply.

2. There are three dice in the cup. Roll the dice.

3. Place the highest die on the side. Put the other two

dice back in the cup and roll again.

4. Place the higher die on the side with the first die, and roll the third die again.

5. Figure out your score: Add the first two dice, and multiply this sum by the number on the third die.

6. Record your results on the Class Score Sheet. We will see who got the highest score. (If high scores are tied, there will be a run-off.)

DICE-A-MATHICS CLASS SCORE SHEET					
NAME	DIE # 1	DIE # 2	SUBTOTAL	DIE # 3	SCORE

STATION 10   **Spellbound**

1. Turn on the tape recorder. You will hear a word, then a sentence with the word in it, then the word repeated.

2. Take a sheet of paper. Write the numbers 1 - 20 in a column.

3. Listen to each sentence. Write the spelling words on your paper.

4. Use the dictionary to check your work. Correct any errors you may have made.

5. Put your paper in the basket.

Discussion

Before initiating this center, the teacher should briefly explain the learning-centered approach to the class. The students should be told that they will be moving about the room working at various centers or stations independently, at their own rates. They should understand the procedures to be followed, and know what to do if they don't understand something. Establish rules for movement that avoid unnecessary noise and confusion.

As children work at their tasks, the teacher can move around the room answering questions, making suggestions, becoming acquainted, establishing relationships.

Feel free to alter, delete or add stations in order to more closely fit the level of your group. Other stations that might be included are: clay modeling, the weekly schedule, predictions and goals for the year, designing covers for individual folders, making a fall collage, etc. The teacher might designate himself as a center and have children interview him. Academic centers may be added, providing preliminary diagnostic data which may be used for making plans for direct teaching and for creating other learning centers. One teacher made up a Math Quiz checking on the work of the previous year. The results furnished the teacher with diagnostic information that could be used for program planning, and also indicated to the students that learning centers are for enjoyment and work.

Rhyming Words

LEARNING CENTER NO. 2   LANGUAGE ARTS   LEVEL K-1

BUTTERFLY HUNT

For the Student

Objective
You will make butterflies by putting together a body and wings that belong to the same rhyming word family.

Materials
You will need: writing paper, pencil, scissors, construction paper, magic marker, crayons.

---

*Developed from ideas contributed by Shirley Engel.

Directions

1. Take a butterfly body out of the pocket. Say the word family out loud to yourself.

2. Look in the Butterfly Wings pocket. Each wing has a picture on it. Find the two large wings and the two small wings that go with the body you picked. Say the words for the pictures out loud to yourself. Do they rhyme with the word family on the body? If they do, fasten the wings to the body (large wings on top, small ones on bottom.)

3. Take another butterfly body and find the matching wings for it. Repeat until you have used all the pieces in the envelopes.

Evaluation

Take an Answer Sheet and a Record Sheet from the Evaluation pocket.

Check your work by matching your completed butterflies with the ones on the answer sheet. Did you get them all right?

Fill out the Record Sheet and put it in your folder.

On Your Own

1. Try to complete the Butterfly Word Families form. Write the words for each picture in each word family. If you can think of more words that go in the family, write them down too. Put the paper in your folder.

2. Make a new butterfly body using construction paper. Think up a new word family and write it on the body with a magic marker. Make two large wings and two small wings to go with the body. On each wing draw a picture of a word that belongs to your word family. Show your work to your teacher. Maybe he will add it to the center for other children to work at.

Suggestions for the Teacher—Learning Center No. 2

Objective

Learning to recognize and sound out members of a word

family is an important beginning reading skill. The child who is learning to associate sounds, or auditory symbols, with letters, or written symbols, will enjoy seeing how the entire image can change when just one sound element changes. This exercise offers reinforcement of beginning phonics skills in an appealing fashion.

Directions for Making the Center

1. Use colorful posterboard to construct this center. Write the title at the top of the board (Butterfly Hunt). Draw a picture of an animal holding a butterfly net. (Young children readily identify with animals.)

2. Using construction paper, cut out eight bodies, 16 large wings and 16 small wings.

3. Write a word family on each body part with magic markers.

4. Draw pictures on the wing pieces for each word family. If you are a reluctant artist, you will find old workbooks or dictionaries excellent sources for small pictures which you can copy or cut out and mount.

5. Laminate all butterfly parts.

6. Using pipe cleaner, attach feelers to the tops of the body parts.

7. Paste bits of velcro along the body parts and on the wings.

8. Prepare Answer Sheets, Record Sheets, On Your Own Sheets. Be sure to check children's work. Whenever possible, add children's independent work to the center. These children can serve as advisors to others working here.

Discussion

Before doing this center, the children will have played rhyming games under the direction of their teacher. (e.g. "With my eye, I spy. . . . something in this room that rhymes with *hair*." "With my eye, I spy. . . . something in the sky that rhymes with *spoon*.")

They should also be familiar with the term "word families" from games and exercises. (e.g. Each child selects a picture card from a deck. They pin the picture to their clothes and then walk around the room, joining others to form small groups of rhyming word families.)

This center could also be used for a math center by putting combinations on the wing pieces and numbers on the body pieces. These can be simple or difficult and are adaptable to all levels.

The same idea could also be used for a more advanced center in the language arts, using butterfly bodies for word roots, and the wings for prefixes or suffixes (for example: -tract: sub-, con-, de-, re-; ped-: -al, -estal, -estrian, -igree).

Vowel Sounds

LEARNING CENTER NO. 3   LANGUAGE ARTS LEVELS 1-2

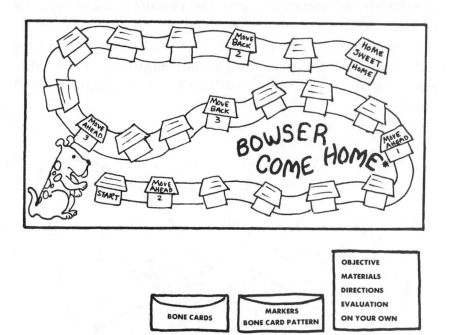

BOWSER, COME HOME

For the Student

Objective

You will play a game which will show how well you know your short and long vowels.

Materials

You will need: magazines, scissors, construction paper, paste, magic markers, game markers.

---

*Developed from ideas contributed by Sharon Guarente.

Directions

1. Find one, two or three friends to play this game with. Choose who goes first, second, third, fourth by using a choosing rhyme. (e.g. I like chocolate, and you do, too. I choose Y-O-U.)

2. Each player takes a different color game marker from the pocket.

3. Take all the Bone Cards from the envelope. Shuffle them and put them picture side up on the game board.

4. The first player takes the top card. Look at the picture, and say the word.

5. Say what vowel is in the word.

6. Spell the word.

7. Turn the bone card over. See if you got the vowel sound right, and if you spelled the word right.

8. If you got the vowel sound right, move the number of spaces it tells you on the card. If incorrect, stay where you are.

9. If you spelled the word right, move one more space.

10. If the house you land on gives you directions, follow them.

11. Put the card on the bottom of the pile.

12. Each player does the same in turn.

13. The first player to reach Home wins.

14. Put all the bone cards back in the envelope.

Evaluation

You will check your own and each others' work by looking on the back of each bone card.

On Your Own

Make new bone cards. Take the bone card pattern from the pocket. Take a sheet of construction paper. Trace the bone many times; then cut out the bone forms.

Get some magazines. Cut out pictures to mount on the bones.

Paste each picture on a bone card. On the back of the bone card, write the word and the vowel. Tell how many spaces to move.

Show your work to your teacher. Maybe he will add your cards to the bone pile.

Example:

Front   Back

Suggestions for the Teacher—Learning Center No. 3

Objectives

One of the early steps in developing phonics skills is differentiating long and short vowels. Children need practice identifying vowel sounds. One way to provide such practice is to make use of easy-to-make games. This center asks children to identify long and short vowels and relate the vowel sound to its spelling in the word.

The center also gives children an opportunity to use manual skills in tracing, cutting, pasting, writing.

Directions for Making the Center

1. This center should be placed on a table.

2. Next to the gameboard on the table, place a folder or envelope for the Objective, Materials, Directions, Evaluation, and On Your Own.

3. On a piece of posterboard draw a series of about 20 dog houses in an S-shaped path. Write the title, "Bowser, Come Home."

4. Draw a place for the bone cards on the posterboard and label it.

5. Draw Bowser and write *Start* under him.

6. Write *Home, Sweet, Home* on the last house.

7. Write directions on a few of the houses to Move Ahead or Move Back and how many spaces.

8. Using oaktag cut out 30 bones. Also, make a pattern for the On Your Own activity.

9. On the front of each bone, paste or draw a picture representing a word you think your children can spell and can identify its vowel sound.

10. Next to the picture, write directions for how many spaces to move. Reward the more difficult words with bigger moves.

11. On the back, write out the whole word, and give the vowel.

Example:

Front   Back

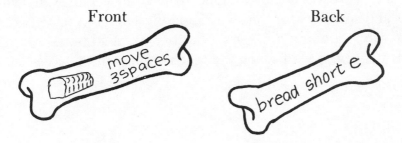

12. Suggested words for bone cards and number of spaces to move:

long a	*long e*	*long i*	*long o*	*long u*
play 1	bee 1	cry 1	bow 1	moon 1
cane 2	key 2	tie 2	rose 2	shoe 2
nail 3	needle 3	bride 3	boat 3	blue 3

short a	*short e*	*short i*	*short o*	*short u*
hat 1	red 1	fish 1	top 1	sun 1
happy 2	belt 2	kick 2	box 2	bug 2
crab 3	bread 3	clip 3	clock 3	jump 3

13. Place the bone cards in an envelope near the gameboard on the table.

14. Put another envelope near the gameboard with the bone card pattern. Include four different colored markers (chips, buttons).

Discussion

The center assumes that children have been previously introduced to long and short vowels through rhyming games and other exercises. It simply provides a fun way to reinforce this skill and to provide additional practice.

It allows children to demonstrate their recognition of long and short vowels, and then to use their knowledge to select appropriate pictures.

The center can be expanded in several directions. The pictures and words may be changed to introduce more difficult words and spellings for the short and long vowels (see Milk the Vowel Cow, Learning Center Number 4). Additional vowel sounds may be added when the teacher finds these have been mastered.

Long and Short Vowels

LEARNING CENTER NO. 4   LANGUAGE ARTS LEVELS 2-3

MILK THE VOWEL COW

For the Student

Objective
You will sort words according to long and short vowel sounds.

Materials
You will need: pencil, magic marker, magazines, scissors, construction paper, paste.

---

*Developed from ideas contributed by Sharon Guarente.

Directions

1. Take a milk bottle picture card from the milk can. Say the name of the picture to yourself.

2. Decide if you hear a long or short vowel sound in the first syllable of the word.

3. Decide which vowel you hear.

4. Place your milk bottle card in the vowel sound pail which represents the sound you hear.

5. Take a Score Sheet from the pocket. Write the word for the picture in the column where you think it belongs.

6. Do the same with each milk bottle picture card.

Evaluation

1. Take the Answer Key from the pocket. Compare your Score Sheet with the Answer Key. (You may want to check the words with the pictures you put in each pail.)

2. Add up your score. Give yourself one point for each picture you put in the right pail. Give yourself two points for each word you spelled right.

3. Mix up the milk bottle cards and put them back in the milk can.

4. Put your Score Sheet in your folder. Your teacher will go over it with you during your conference.

On Your Own

Make your own Vowel Album. Take 10 pieces of construction paper. You may choose whatever colors you like.

At the top of each sheet of construction paper write the name of the vowel (e.g. long e, short e, etc.). Cut pictures out of magazines and paste them on the sheet of construction paper where they belong.

Cut small strips of white paper. Write the word for each picture you posted in your album on a separate strip. On the back of each strip, write the vowel for the word.

Make a cover for your Vowel Album. Decorate it so it looks attractive. Put your name on it.

On the inside of the cover, paste an envelope large enough to hold your word strips.

Invite a classmate to take the words out of the envelope, identify the vowel, and find the picture.

Show your Album to your teacher.

Suggestions for the Teacher—Learning Center No. 4

Objectives

Many children find it rather easy to identify initial and final consonant sounds in words. Identifying vowel sounds is a more difficult task because of the irregularities in English spelling. This center will provide additional practice in mastering this skill. The approach offers an interesting change-of-pace activity from the usual worksheet in phonics books.

The center also gives children the chance to apply their knowledge to create materials of their own.

Directions for Making the Center

1. Mount this center on a large posterboard. Draw a cow in the center and print the name of the center on top.

2. Use 10 dixie cups or pint ice-cream containers. Label each with the name of the vowel. Staple each cup to the posterboard, arranging the five long vowel cups on the left side of the cow, and the five short vowel cups on the right.

3. Cut out 40 cards shaped like milk bottles. Draw or paste pictures on the cards, four pictures for each vowel. Cut the cards to a size that will fit into the cups or containers.

4. Run off Score Sheets and put them in a pocket on the center.

5. Prepare an Answer Key card. Laminate it and put it in a pocket on the center.

Milk the Vowel Cow Score Sheet

_____   _____
          Name   *Date*

long a	long e	long i	long o	long u

short a	short e	short i	short o	short u

Number of words I classified under the right vowel _____
Number of words I spelled right _____ x 2 = _____

MY TOTAL SCORE: _____

Milk the Vowel Cow Answer Sheet

long a	long e	long i	long o	long u
baby	green bean	violin	yoyo	bugle
reindeer	beach	firefly	hose	suit
crayon	leaves	ninety	notebook	newspaper
rainbow	shield	tiger	soldier	student or pupil

short a	short e	short i	short o	short u
rabbit	letter	hippo	socks	butter
jacket	telephone	mittens	rocket	puppet
laugh	melon	slippers	doctor	money
raccoon	feather	whistle	monster	monkey

Discussion

This center is an extension of Learning Center Number 3, Bowser, Come Home. It illustrates additional game techniques for advancing phonics skills which require much independent practice.

This center can easily be increased or decreased in difficulty, according to the level of the children in the class, by changing the pictures on the milk bottles.

If the teacher thinks it would be necessary or helpful, he may write the word for each picture on the back of the milk bottle cards.

Feelings

LEARNING CENTER NO. 5   LANGUAGE ARTS LEVELS 2-4

TELL ABBY HOW YOU FEEL

For the Student

Objective

You will have activities and games that will help you to be sensitive to the many feelings people have.

You will learn the names for the different feelings that we all feel at different times.

You will share some of your feelings and experiences.

Materials

You will need: paper, pencils, tape recorder, scissors, paste, old magazines and newspapers, construction paper, mirror, clay.

Directions

1. Under the picture of Abby are four faces. Choose the one that closest describes how you feel today. Use the tape recorder, or if you wish you may write, to tell why you feel this way. Let a friend hear your tape or read your paper. Discuss it with him. Use this scale to tell how you feel after the discussion.

1	2	3	4
Worse	The same	A little better	Much better

2. Turn the spinner at the center. Read the word on which it stops. Write or tape a story that tells about something that happened to you that made you feel that way. If you cannot think of an experience on your own, think of something that happened to someone you know, or something you read in a story or saw on TV.

Share your story with a friend. Tell about his reaction. Check one or more of these sentences:

He liked my story.
He felt sorry for me.

He had an experience like the one I told about.

He thought I was right.

He thought I was wrong.

3. Take the Feelings Pictures from the pocket. Arrange them in order from happy to sad. (Put the picture of Abby aside.)

4. Take the Feelings Words from the pocket. Match each picture with a word. Put the word card under the picture card it belongs with. Check your own work. Turn over each pair of cards. On the back, you will see a tab. Lift the tab. See if the number on the picture card is the same as the number on the word card you matched it with.

5. Get a friend to join you in some games. Take all the picture cards and all the word cards. Shuffle them together. Play Concentration. Put all the cards face down in rows. Take turns turning over any two cards. If they are a pair, keep them. If not, turn them face down again. See who wins the most pairs.

Play Old Maid or Go Fish. Use the Abby Card and all the picture and word cards. See who gets left with the Abby Card after all the pairs are laid down.

If you want to check to see if you are right when you match a picture and a word, look at the numbers under the tabs. If they are the same, you are right.

Put all the cards back in their pockets.

6. Take the Feeling Words from the pocket. Lay them out in a row in front of you. Take one of the Feelings Situation Cards from the pocket. Read it. How would you feel if that situation happened to you? Lay the Situation Card under the Feeling Word.

Do the same with all the other Feelings Situation Cards. When you have finished, you should have two Situation Cards under each Feeling Word. Show your work to a classmate or to your teacher.

Evaluation

You and your classmates will check your own work.

Your teacher will also look at your work.

On Your Own

1. Look at yourself in the mirror. Make a happy face, a sad face, a

worried face, a lonely face. Make faces that show other feelings. Take a piece of paper. Copy these sentences and complete them. Then put your paper in your folder.

I feel happy when_____.

I feel angry when _____.

I feel lonely when _____.

I feel loved when _____.

I feel frustrated when_____.

2. Make a feelings booklet. Find some old magazines and newspapers. Cut out pictures that show feelings. Cut out as many pictures as you can. Put the pictures in groups according to the feeling they show. Paste all the pictures that show the same feeling on a sheet of construction paper. Write the name of that feeling at the top of the sheet. Make a page for each group of pictures that show the same feeling. Make a cover for your booklet and staple it together. Show it to your class.

3. Using modeling clay, make some mood dolls. Show how each one feels.

- Make one look happy.
- Make one look sad.
- Make one look angry.
- Make one look afraid.
- Make any other to look any way you wish.

When you have finished, write the word that tells how each doll feels and stick it to the doll. Put your dolls on the table.

Suggestions for the Teacher—Learning Center No. 5

Objectives
The activities at this center encourage children to become aware of

how they feel and to express their feelings. As they engage in the activities, and discuss their feelings with their classmates and the teacher, they should recognize that people feel differently at different times and that it is legitimate to have unpleasant feelings at times.

The center also furnishes the teacher the opportunity to become more aware of children's feelings. This permits the teacher to deal more appropriately with children.

Providing children with the vocabulary of emotions, and demonstrating that an open and honest expression of ideas and feelings is legitimate, are very important steps toward self-understanding and toward understanding and sympathizing with others.

Suggestions for Making the Center

1. Use posterboard as the background for the center. Mount it on a bulletin board or room divider. Write the heading on the posterboard or cut out letters for forming it. Draw the picture of Abby (or any other character).

2. Draw happy, sad, angry, afraid faces on posterboard, oaktag, or construction paper of a color that contrasts with the background and mount them to the center.

3. Make a spinner from a piece of contrasting posterboard. Divide it into six sections and write a feeling word in each section. Mount the spinner to the circle with a brad. Place two metal washers over the brad, one underneath the spinner, one on top of it so that it spins more easily. (If this doesn't work well when mounted vertically, you can make a spinner using a margarine container with a plastic top. Divide the top into six sections, write a feeling word in each, and pin the spinner in the middle.)

4. Make a pocket for the Feelings Words. Use index cards or pieces of oaktag the size of regular playing cards. Using a flair pen or magic marker write words such as these on the cards: happy, sad, embarrassed, disappointed, angry, afraid, excited (eager), frustrated, lonely, worried, loved.

5. Make a pocket for the Feelings Pictures. Use index cards or pieces of oaktag the same size as the word cards. Draw or cut out and paste pictures for the feelings on each card. The samples given here

have the words under them for identification only. Your picture cards should not have identifying words.

6. On the back of each picture card and word card pair, write the same number. Order the numbers from happy to sad as in Directions for Children. Cover the numbers with tabs that the children can lift for self-checking.

HAPPY	LONELY	WORRIED
ANGRY	ABBY	AFRAID
LOVED	SAD	FRUSTRATED
DISAPPOINTED	EMBARRASSED	EXCITED

7. Make a pocket for the Feelings Situation Cards. On strips of oaktag describe briefly two situations for each feeling.

SUGGESTED SITUATION CARDS:

Angry	Your brother or sister takes your ice cream. Your mother throws out your favorite toy.
Happy	Your best friend is spending the night with you. You open your birthday present.
Sad	Your pet dog dies. Your best friend is sick.
Lonely	No one is home with you. You went to the playground but no one is there.
Afraid	You hear a loud, strange noise. You see a snake in the yard.
Worried	You have to go to the dentist for a check up. Your mother is in the hospital.
Disappointed	You didn't get what you wanted for your birthday. You were supposed to go on a picnic but it rained.
Loved	Your mother kisses you. Your puppy licks you on the face.
Excited/ Eager	Tomorrow is Christmas Day. Your father said he'd take you to see "The Pink Panther Show."
Frustrated	You don't have time to finish watching your favorite TV show.

You can't fit all your books in your school bag.

Embarrassed   Your pants tore while you were playing baseball.
                   Your teacher scolded you in class.

8. Provide all the materials needed, as well as display and bulletin board space for children's creations.

Discussion

The center may be made more or less difficult by changing the feelings words. It could be made an on-going experience by starting with a few words and adding one or two continually. A feelings center can be used at every grade level by introducing appropriate words and concepts. At older levels more difficult words can be used (such as depressed, downcast, irritable, etc.). More subtle concepts—for example, mixed emotions, feeling one way and pretending to feel another, irrational feelings such as prejudice, etc.—may be handled through appropriate activities. Also, activities can be planned to explore different ways of dealing with feelings.

The products children produce at this center are important, but they are not nearly as important as the self-image which they project. The teacher should be sure to schedule time for class discussions and conferences so that feelings can be talked out and concepts clarified.

Some children might not be happy making the clay doll models. Suggest that they may make models of cowboys, policemen, or such. It may be necessary to demonstrate the making of a doll model to show that feelings can be shown in the face and in the whole body.

Although some answers and self-checking devices are provided, there are really no right or wrong answers. Children may identify a feeling or situation as anger which you have labeled something else (embarrassment, frustration). This is all right as long as it is clear that the child knows the various emotion words and is really differing in opinion or judgment. The important thing is that there be open discussion of feelings.

Poetry

LEARNING CENTER NO. 6   LANGUAGE ARTS LEVELS 3-6

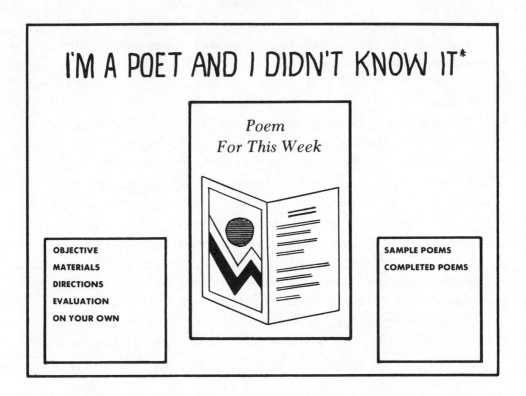

I'M A POET AND I DIDN'T KNOW IT

For the Student

Objective

To create simple poems to express an idea or create an image in concise, poetic language.

Materials

You will need paper, magic markers, flair pens, water colors, poetry books.

---

*Developed from ideas contributed by Joan Carlson.

Directions

1. Read the sample Poem for This Week. You can find some other samples in the Sample Poems pocket.

2. Study the poem and try to figure out its form. The basic structure is very simple; it's a whole story told in as few words as possible. The first line tells Who; the second line tells What; the third line tells When; the fourth line tells Where; and the fifth line tells Why. (Variations may be made. For example, the third and fourth lines may be interchanged.)

3. Find a private place and try to write your own poem using this simple pattern.

4. Make an illustration to accompany your poem. Use water colors, magic markers, flair pens, pencils, or any other materials you like.

5. Put your poem and your illustration (with your name on them) in the Completed Poems pocket.

Evaluation

Make a list of contrasting adjectives, such as:

warm	cool		bubbly	still
smooth	rough		calm	excited
sharp	round		mint green	chocolate brown
noisy	quiet		heavy	delicate

Circle the word in each pair that you would associate with your poem.

Show or read your poem to a friend. Then read each word pair to your friend. Ask him to choose the word in each pair that he associates with your poem. Compare his answers with your own. Sometimes people have very different reactions, and sometimes they agree. It is interesting to try to see where and how we are similar or different in our responses. What did you find out about your poem?

On Your Own

Pretend you work for a greeting card company. Use this

formula for creating a poem for some special occasion.

Write a poem using this structure for a member of your family. Give or mail it to him.

Put copies of any poems you write in the Completed Poems pocket.

Suggestions for the Teacher—Learning Center No. 6

Objective

People often shy away from poetry as something unfamiliar or difficult. Yet each person has within him the capacity to experience life with a poet's eye. The purpose of introducing children to the writing of simple, structured poems is to give them easy access to the sensitivity of poetry.

It is easy to create a poem in this structured way, and this is a first step toward the appreciation of the poet's craft. A whole world of esthetic and intellectual stimulation can open up and become available.

Children with special talents in this area should be encouraged to read widely and to experiment freely with many different forms.

Directions for Making the Center

1. Use posterboard or cardboard that has been painted or covered with colored contact paper to construct the center.

2. Write the sample poem on a piece of colored paper that contrasts with the background. Insert it into slits in the cardboard; or attach it with velcro; or use any other means that easily allows for the periodic changing of material mounted.

3. Illustrate the poem, realistically or abstractly, creating a card.

4. Include several samples in the pocket.

5. Have many books of poetry available at the center, as well as samples of students' works.

6. Sample poems:

My kid brother
Jumped for joy
When he woke up this morning,
Saw a puppy on his bed
And knew it was his birthday present.

I
Feel joyful
When I see a child
Toddle down the street
To his Daddy.

The man
Trudged slowly
Home
That evening
Dreading what he would find.

Eating
Popcorn
At the movies
All through the show
Is nice.

Discussion

Before the writing of poems is introduced into a learning center, the children need a sequence of group experiences with careful teacher guidance. Starting with exercises that are highly structured makes for a gratifying and successful experience. However, student potential is quite unlimited, and both formal and informal experiences should be introduced.

Writing poems is one avenue toward the appreciation of poetry. Reading poems is another. To transmit the beauty of both thought and expression, and the special linguistic crafts of the poet, the teacher and students should do a lot of listening to and reading of poetry.

Some very helpful books are available to the teacher who wants to expose students to the poetic experience. Two outstanding books are those by Kenneth Koch, *Wishes, Lies and Dreams*, New York, Random, 1971, and *Rose, Where Did You Get That Red?*, New York, Random, 1974. Another very fine book is *My Sister Looks Like A Pear* by Douglas Anderson, New York, Hart, 1974.

The teacher should change the forms and the samples in the learning center periodically. A wide variety of structured forms lend themselves to this kind of student creativity, e.g. haiku, cinquain, tanka, couplet, triplet, quatrain, limerick, concrete, diamond, onomatopoeia. There are also many ingenious suggestions for less structured activities in the books recommended above.

The teacher should be sure to give positive recognition to the poems written by students working at this center. A poetry reading session may be held, or a book of the students' poems may be mimeographed and distributed.

Poetry is designed to be read aloud. If the classroom is equipped with tape recorders, students may record their poems instead of (or in addition to) writing them.

A Researched Speech

LEARNING CENTER NO. 7   LANGUAGE ARTS LEVELS 4 AND UP

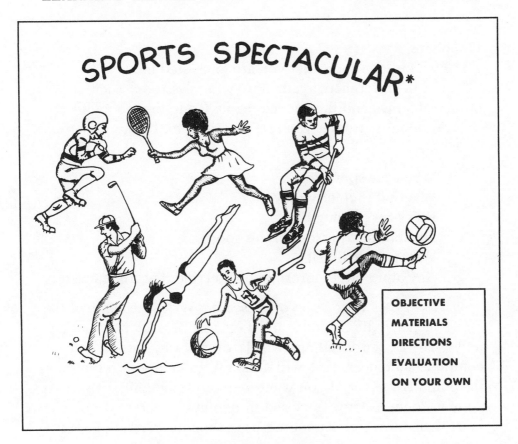

SPORTS SPECTACULAR

For the Student

Objective

To prepare a brief speech about some sport based on data you researched yourself.

---

*Developed from ideas contributed by Joanne Damadio.

Materials

You will need *Sports Almanac*, encyclopedias, library books, cassette recorder.

Directions

1. Pick out one sport that you are interested in.

2. Use the references available in your classroom, such as: the *Sports Almanac* and the encyclopedia. Go to the school library for additional sources if you feel you need to. Look up matters such as:

> When the sport began
> Where it is chiefly played
> Rules for playing it
> Outstanding persons in this sport
> Why people like it
> Any other bits of information you find that are interesting

3. Take notes as you do your research. Write the name of the reference, including volume and page numbers, at the top. Your notes can be informal, in words or phrases rather than in complete sentences. Just write enough to help you remember the point. However, if you want to quote something, be sure to copy it down exactly, enclosed in quotation marks. If you use more than one reference source, use a separate card or paper for your notes from each source.

4. Look through all your notes and organize them logically or chronologically, according to your subject. Making an outline of the major topics helps to keep your ideas in sequence.

5. Prepare a brief talk, five to ten minutes long. Your talk will be clear if you follow some kind of outline. But to make your talk interesting, think about a good opening sentence. Perhaps you can introduce your subject by presenting one of the most interesting things you learned in doing your research; or perhaps you can tell how you came to be interested in this particular sport.

6. Using the cassette recorder, record your talk. Then label the tape with your name and topic.

Evaluation

When everyone has completed this center, we will have a Sports Spectacular. Everyone will play his tape for the class so we can learn as much about each sport as possible.

After the Sports Spectacular, a class discussion will be conducted. We will share our reactions to the speeches and talk about what made the talks interesting and informative.

On Your Own

Do as many of the following suggested activities as you wish. Post your completed work on the Sports bulletin board for other students to read.

1. Pretend you are the sports columnist for your school newspaper. Write up a game or match your school team participated in.

2. Pretend you are the sports columnist for the local daily newspaper. Write up a sports event for the column, or a special feature story about some player.

3. Pretend you are a TV sports commentator. You are covering a live sports event, reporting it blow by blow, including audience responses. Tape record your running comments.

4. Write a fan letter to your favorite sports hero. (Mail it if you like; you may be surprised to receive an answer.)

5. Interview your gym teacher, or the coach of one of your school teams, about some controversial sports topic, such as: spectator versus participant sports, individual versus team competition in sports, mixing sexes on ball teams.

Suggestions for the Teacher—Learning Center No. 7

Objectives

Basing some of our conversation on researched facts and

information is an important skill to develop. Knowing which reference sources to use for a specific purpose, taking notes, outlining and organizing data are promoted here through a highly motivated activity.

Being able to present information in an interesting way is an important social skill. Giving only facts can be as boring as speaking in generalities without data. A good conversationalist and a convincing speaker can blend facts and ideas into an interesting whole.

Directions for Making the Center

1. Make the center on posterboard or cardboard that has been covered with colored contact or construction paper.

2. Select colorful pictures from magazines, such as *Sports Illustrated*. Mount them in a collage-like fashion. (Your students might be asked to make this collage.)

3. If your school does not provide cassette recorders and tapes, students might be asked to bring in their own. Several talks might be recorded on the same tape. If no recorders are available, the Sports Spectacular will have to be held live.

4. The classroom should be stocked with a variety of reference sources. If your school library does not allow students free access at all times, arrange with the librarian for your students to be allowed to use the library upon presentation of a written note.

Discussion

Doing research is a highly complex skill involving many sub-skills, such as being familiar with the various reference sources and with what they contain and how they are organized, using a library card file, using an index and table of contents, note taking, making an outline, etc. Each of these skills may be worked on independently before a topic which combines them all is tackled. However, it is more interesting to students to do real research on topics that interest them than to do mechanical exercises that build component skills. The teacher has to use his ingenuity in creating tasks and activities that build up these important research skills in gradual succession.

This particular activity may be done by students in small groups. After they make their selection of sports, those who have chosen the same sport may combine their research and reporting efforts. The topic is easily broken down, and different students may handle different aspects, making a combined presentation at the end.

Other subjects, such as topics in science or social studies, e.g. animals, trees, vehicles, disease and its cure, may be treated in this same way. The more opportunities students have to do their own research and to report orally on their results, the more effective will they become as scholars and conversationalists.

Bulletin boards for various subjects (Sports, Literature, Current Events, etc.) should be a permanent part of the classroom, or mounted on walls in corridors just outside the classroom. Displaying the work of students encourages more and more independent efforts.

Mystery Stories

LEARNING CENTER NO. 8   LANGUAGE ARTS LEVELS 5-6

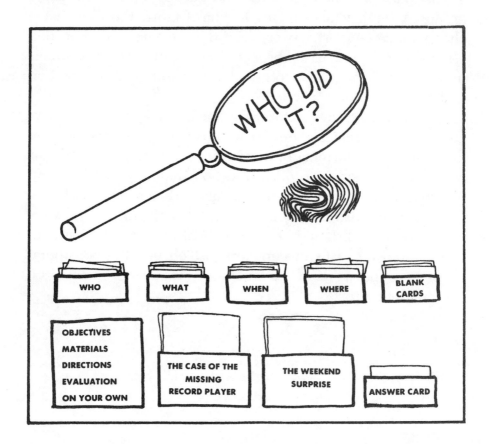

WHO DID IT?

For the Student

Objective
    You will see how good you are at using and creating clues.
    You will learn how to write a mystery story.

Materials
    You will need: pencil, paper.

Directions

1. Look at these series and see if you can figure out what comes next. Write your answer in the blank.

   a. 2, 4, 6, 8, 10, _____

   b. 1, 2, 4, 8, 16, 32, _____

   c. 3, 8, 13, 18, 23, _____

   d. 5, 6, 8, 11, 15, 20, _____

   e. 4, 5, 8; 6, 7, 12; 7, 8, _____

   f. C, F, I, L, O, _____

   g. apple, bread, corn, doughnut, egg, _____

   h. hot, cold, young, old, stale, _____

   i. happy, glad, present, gift, perhaps, _____

   j. two, too, ate, eight, sale, _____

Take the answer card from the pocket and check your work.

2. You used clues to solve some problems in Activity 1. A good mystery story makes use of clues. There are three basic elements that make a mystery story exciting, interesting and mysterious:

   a. The *characters*—Each person must be described vividly. They have to seem real. Using direct quotations to let them speak for themselves helps.

   b. The *style*—Details must be clear. The words should be carefully chosen to make the reader interested.

   c. The *plot*—The essential parts of the plot are:

   (1) The MYSTERY—This part tells what the mystery is, when and where it happened, to whom it happened, and who else was involved. The mystery may be written about many different situations—a robbery, a surprise, a missing person, animal, or object, an un-

usual noise or happening, a murder, a peculiar disease, etc.

(2) The CLUES—This part tells some details that allow the mystery to be figured out. Clues might be provided by a letter, a piece of clothing, a wallet or some other personal possession, fingerprints, footprints, or tire tracks, a smell or taste, a sound, etc.

(3) The SOLUTION—Someone figures out the mystery.

(4) The ENDING—This part tells what happened after the mystery was solved.

3. Take the sample mystery story, "The Case of the Missing Record Player," from the pocket. Read it carefully. When you finish reading the story, get a sheet of paper and answer these questions:

a. What did you like best about the story? Rank these three elements by putting 1 next to the thing you liked best, 3 next to the weakest element.

_____ characters
_____ style
_____ plot

b. What was the mystery?

c. What was the clue?

d. What was the solution?

e. What was the ending?

Show your answers to a classmate who completed this center. If you do not agree, discuss it with the teacher.

4. Now read another mystery story, "The Weekend Surprise." After reading the story, get a sheet of paper and answer these questions:

a. Rank these three elements to show what you liked best about the story and what you liked least:

_____ characters
_____ style
_____ plot

b. What was the mystery?

c. What were the clues?

d. What was the solution?

e. What was the ending?

f. Which story did you like better—"The Missing Record Player" or "The Weekend Surprise?" Why? Show and discuss your answers with a classmate who completed this center. If you do not agree, find a third classmate and discuss it together.

5. There are several mystery story books at the center. You may want to read one or more of these before continuing.

6. Now it's time to write your own mystery story. On the center are four pockets labeled: WHO, WHAT, WHEN, WHERE. Take one card from each pocket. Study the four cards. Use them to form a plot for your own original mystery story. Make up the mystery, the clues, the solution, and the ending for a story based upon your four cards. If you can't come up with an idea, you may try exchanging one of your cards with another card from the same pocket. Get a sheet of paper and write the words that are on your cards at the top of the paper. Then replace the cards in their pockets. Write your mystery story. Take your time. Think it out. It may take you several days to write a story you like.

Evaluation

Find a partner and read all but the ending of your story to him.

See if he can solve the mystery. Then read him the ending. See if he likes the way you solved your mystery. Rewrite any parts of your story you think you can improve. Put your finished product on the Mystery Stories bulletin board.

On Your Own

1. Make up a set of *who, what, when,* and *where* words that could be used to stimulate a plot for a mystery story. Write each on one of the blank cards you will find in the pocket. Using the words you wrote on the blank cards, make up a new mystery story. Place it on the Mystery Stories bulletin board. Put your *who, what, when,* and *where* cards in the pockets at the center. Perhaps someone in your class will choose your words and you will be able to compare your stories.

2. Get a mystery story book from the school or classroom library. Read the story and make a set of *who, what, when* and *where* cards for it. Show your cards to a classmate who has not read the book. Get him to tell you a mystery story based on the words. Discuss with him the differences in the two stories.

3. Pair up with a friend. Select one set of *who, what, when* and *where* words from the pockets. Write a story together based on these words. See if you think it is easier to write a story with someone than writing it alone. See if you think the story you wrote together was more interesting than the story you wrote alone. Put the story on the bulletin board.

4. Look out of a window from which you can observe people walking on the street or driving past in cars or trucks. Observe them carefully. Use your imagination and write a mystery story based upon what you see.

Suggestions for the Teacher—Learning Center No. 8

Objectives

This center furnishes a splendid opportunity to blend reading and writing skills. Understanding *who, what, when,* and *where* is a comprehension skill that is introduced at the beginning reading levels and spirals until mastery is achieved in the upper grades. Many times, children fail to apply these skills to enhance their work in other language areas.

At this center children use their *who, what, when,* and *where* skills to understand a story plot and then write their own stories using the same skills. The activity is both structured and open-ended to allow children to exercise their own creative talents and imagination to whatever extent they can.

Directions for Making the Center

1. Use a real magnifying glass or draw one. Attach it to a large sheet of posterboard or cardboard that has been painted or covered with colored contact or construction paper, or use a bulletin board or room divider as the background for the center.

2. Make and label pockets for the Who, What, When and Where cards; for the two sample mystery stories; for the blank cards; for the answer cards; and for the Objective, Materials, Directions, Evaluation, On Your Own.

3. Mount all nine pockets to the center.

4. Make up an Answer Card for the first activity and put it in the pocket.

Who-Did-It Answer Card

a. 12   Add two to each successive number.

b. 64   Double each successive number (or multiply by 2).

c. 28   Add five to each successive number.

d. 26   Increase each successive number by one more than the previous increment.

e. 14   In each series of three numbers add one to the

first number to get the second number and double the first number to get the third number.

f. R   The third next letter in the alphabet.

g. Any food beginning with the letter *f*.

h. fresh—pairs of antonyms.

i. maybe—pairs of synonyms.

j. sail—pairs of homonyms.

5. Cut oaktag or posterboard into 2″ x 4″ strips or cards. Place some blank cards in the pocket for children to write their own words upon. On the rest of the cards, write words or phrases with a magic marker or flair pen for the Who, What, When, Where pockets. Make about 10 cards for each pocket. Color cue the cards for easy replacement in their correct pockets.

SUGGESTED WORDS:

WHO   Spacemen, wolves, racing car driver, robbers, my father, pilot, artist, witch, my teacher, doctor, dog, rabbit.

WHAT   Robbed a bank, saw a UFO, was lost in the desert, ran from the lion, entered their spaceship, was working on his car, picked up the laser gun, lost his scalpel, was performing surgery, could not find the moon, held up the stagecoach, bit Uncle John.

WHEN   Halloween, last night, a hot summer day, during the hurricane, a cold windy night, 10:00 p.m., two years ago in March, on my birthday, at midnight, before school.

WHERE   In the museum, high in the sky, in the supermarket,

in the elevator, in the backyard, at the race track, on the moon, in the hospital, 30,000 feet in the air, behind my house.

6. Write two mystery stories on oaktag, which you laminate. Put them in the pockets. (Samples given.)

7. Prepare a Mystery Stories bulletin board.

8. Place a number of mystery story books at the center.

SUGGESTED BOOKS:

Nina Bawden, *Squib*, Philadelphia, Lippincott, 1971.
_____, *The Witch's Daughter*, Philadelphia, 1966.
Frank Bonham, *Mystery of the Fat Cat*, New York, Dutton, 1968.
_____, *The Nitty Gritty*, New York, Dutton, 1968.
Scott Corbett, *The Case of the Gone Goose*, Boston, Little, Brown, 1961.
_____, *Run for the Money*, Boston, Little, Brown, 1973.
_____, *Take a Number*, New York, Dutton, 1974.
Peter Dickinson, *The Gift*, Boston, Little, Brown, 1974.
Wilson Gage, *The Secret of Crossbone Hill*, New York, Washington Square Press, 1969.
_____, *The Secret of Indian Mound*, New York, Washington Square Press, 1969.
Jean George, *Who Really Killed Cock Robin?*, New York, Dutton, 1971.
Virginia Hamilton, *The House of Dies Drear*, New York, Macmillan, 1968.
E.W. Hildick, *Manhattan is Missing*, New York, Doubleday, 1969.
Felice Holman, *Elisabeth and the Marsh Mystery*, New York, Macmillan, 1966.
Georgess McHargue, *Funny Bananas: The Mystery at the Museum*, New York, Holt, Rinehart and Winston, 1975.
Donald Sobol, Encyclopedia Brown Series (*Encyclopedia Brown Lends a Hand; Encyclopedia Brown Takes a Case; Encyclopedia Brown Gets His Man; Encyclopedia Brown Strikes Again; Encyclopedia Brown Finds the Clues;* etc.) Nashville, Tenn., Nelson.
Phyllis Whitney, *The Mystery of the Haunted Pool*, Philadelphia, Westminister, 1960.
_____, *Secret of the Emerald Star*, Philadelphia, Westminister, 1964.

Older and more able children might enjoy:

John Buchan, *The Thirty-Nine Steps*, New York, Dutton.
R.C. Bull, editor, *Great Tales of Mystery*, New York, Hill and Wang.
G.K. Chesterton, *The Father Brown Omnibus*, New York, Dodd.
Sir Arthur Conan Doyle, *The Adventures of Sherlock Holmes*, New York, Harper.
Edgar Allen Poe, *Tales*, New York, Dodd.

Some children might like the Nancy Drew, Bobbsey Twins, and Hardy Boys series. The "History Mysteries" stories in the weekly *Junior Scholastic* might also be used as part of this center, and the mini-mysteries from Solve-A-Crime by A.C. Gordon, Singer Features, are very good.

The Case of the Missing Record Player

Bill Stover opened his front door and went straight to his room. It was Friday and it had been a hard but good week at school. His fourth grade teacher had been very pleased with the radio show he had written and his classmates had enjoyed it too.

He was eager to listen again to the new records he had received for his birthday yesterday. "Good grief!" he exclaimed as he looked in amazement at his room. "My record player is missing!"

His mother hadn't seen it. Neither had his father, nor his brother, nor his sister. Someone must have stolen it!

Carefully, Bill began to examine his room. Nothing else was missing and nothing was out of place. The robber had to have gotten in someway. How?

Just then he noticed that the window beside his bed was open. He never ever left that window open when he went to school.

He looked out the window. A white object was lying on the grass. It was too far to the ground to reach it so he sped out the front door and around the house. Picking up the object, he saw it was a man's handkerchief. In the corner were the initials DH.

Bill's father called the police station to report what had happened. The policeman said he would come around to check it out.

Meanwhile, the policeman looked through his files and found that a person named David Harris had robbed some other homes in Bill's neighborhood.

In a half-hour Bill's phone rang. The police had found David Harris with Bill's record player in the trunk of his car.

The case was solved. Bill, proud of his good detective work, spent the entire evening listening to his records.

The Weekend Surprise

The Adams family returned home after an enjoyable weekend at the beach. They quickly unpacked their car and went into the house, eager to get to bed.

As soon as they entered the living room, they realized that something was wrong. A vase that was kept on the mantle was lying broken on the floor. A lamp on the table was lying on its side. The curtain at the front window was torn so that it looked ragged. A picture that had been hanging above the sofa had fallen to the floor.

Everyone was excited. They could find no doors or windows that had been broken into. Nothing seemed to be missing.

Mr. Adams called the police, who arrived in just a few minutes. The officers carefully examined the damaged items as well as the windows and doors. They could find no way that someone had broken into the house.

After a long search, one of the policemen noticed some animal footprints on the piano.

"Do you have a cat?" he asked. "No!" everyone answered.

The policeman said he was sure the damage had to be caused by a small animal that had entered the house and that perhaps it was still inside somewhere.

Just then, they all heard a noise in the kitchen and ran to see what it was. Sitting on the cupboard was a very small squirrel who looked very frightened.

"Open the back door quickly!" shouted one of the policemen. Mr. Adams opened it and out dashed the squirrel. Now they all knew what had caused the damage, but they still didn't know how he had gotten into the house.

"He couldn't have come in through the windows nor the doors," said the policeman. "There is only one other way he could have gotten in, and that's down the chimney."

They all looked into the fireplace. Sure enough, ashes were scattered all over, and a barely noticeable trail of squirrel footprints could be traced into the living room.

The Adams family thanked the policemen for helping them solve the mystery. "We'll have to remember to close the fireplace when we go away again," said Mr. Adams.

"Yes," answered the children, "but we're awfully glad the little squirrel didn't get hurt."

Discussion

Although this center provides a great deal of structure, not all children may be interested or able to work in it. It may be a center designed for only part of the class. Nevertheless, the entire class can profit from sharing the products that come out of the center.

Hold a session in which a number of the stories written by the children are read, discussed and enjoyed. Discuss such details as plot and character development, clues, word choice, logical solutions, and such. Children grow in their writing ability when they interact with others about what they have written.

If it seems appropriate and there is enough interest, perhaps the class can choose the story they liked best. Some of the writers can convert the story into a play, and the class can plan the performance and invite parents to attend.

The framework for this center could easily be adapted to the writing of other story forms—fables, myths, tall tales, and one-act plays.

Poetry

LEARNING CENTER NO. 9   LANGUAGE ARTS LEVELS 5-6

*Developed from ideas contributed by Betty van Arsdale.

SYL-LA-BIC   PO-ET-RY

For the Student

Objectives

Japanese writers have developed many interesting forms of poetry that do not use rhyme. Each poem creates a beautiful image or mood by following specific rules governing the number of lines in the poem, and the number of syllables within each line. You will try writing poems in some of these forms.

You will have much practice in counting the number of syllables in words.

Materials

You will need: paper, dictionary, thesaurus, tape recorder, crayons or paints.

Directions

1. Select one of the poetry forms. Read the sample poems in the pocket for that form. Figure out how many lines there are in that form, how many syllables are used in each line, and the total number of syllables. Record your answers on the Syllabic Poetry form.

2. Select four more poem types and do the same thing.

3. Create a poem of your own for each type you selected. You may use the thesaurus or dictionary to find words you need that have the number of syllables you need.

4. Write or print each of your poems on a separate sheet of paper. Sign them.

5. Illustrate each of your syllabic poems. Put them in the Completed Poems pocket.

6. Return each sample poem to its correct pocket.

Evaluation

1. Use the Syllabic Poetry Answer Sheet to check your work. Or, if the sample poems were written by your classmates, have them check you out.

2. Tape the poems you wrote and play them back to yourself to see if each poem has the correct number of syllables.

3. Get another opinion. Pair up with a friend and have him listen to the tape to see if you followed the syllabic rules.

On Your Own

1. Try the remaining five syllabic poetry forms. Follow the same procedures.

2. Submit your poems to the class or school newspaper.

3. Get together with some other students and make a book of syllabic poetry. Display it on the bulletin board outside your room, or donate it to the school library, or mineograph copies and distribute them to your classmates and other students.

4. Get together with some other students and arrange a poetry reading. Your teacher will clear the time and date for you. Post announcements and invite visitors (parents, aides, administrators, other classes).

Suggestions for the Teacher—Learning Center No. 8

Objectives

Most children are familiar with poems that rhyme. This center acquaints children with a wide variety of unusual, unrhymed poetry. When they see how easy it is to create an image through a few choice words, they become more receptive to poetry and more sensitive to language.

The center also gives practice in the important skill of breaking up words into their component syllables. This is very helpful for reading and spelling.

Directions for Making the Center

1. Use a large sheet of posterboard.

2. Cut the bottom four inches off a brown envelope. Use this bottom part for each pocket. Cut the front of the pocket lower than the back creating a tab. Label each pocket on the tab. Mount the ten pockets on the board.

3. Print or type each poem sample on a 5″ x 8″ index card. Laminate each card or cover it with clear contact paper. Put several sample poems in each pocket to illustrate the form. You may have to create your first samples yourself, but soon the students' original poems will become a rich source of samples. (See samples given below.)

4. Run off forms for Syllabic Poetry and Answer Sheets.

SYLLABIC POETRY			
Form	*# of Lines*	*Total # of Syllables*	*# of Syllables in Each Successive Line*

Syllabic Poetry Answer Sheet			
QUINTET	5	27	3-5-7-9-3
SEPT	7	16	1-2-3-4-3- 2-1
HAIKU	3	17	5-7-5
QUINTAIN	5	30	2-4-6-8-10
CAMEO	7	35	2-5-8-3-8-7-2
CINQUAIN	5	22	2-4-6-8-2
PENSEE	5	27	2-4-7-8-6
TANKA	5	31	5-7-5-7-7
SEPTET	7	39	3-5-7-9-7-5-3
LANTERNE	5	11	1-2-3-4-1

5. Sample syllabic poems*:

QUINTET

Butterflies
Such friendly creatures
Colorful wings on each side
Flit through the air gracefully, settling
On flowers.

SEPT

Bright
Flashing
Shiny green
Spruce, with prickly
Pine needles
And pine
Cones.

HAIKU

Bears licking honey
Sticky paws swatting at bees
Black noses swollen.

QUINTAIN

Mountain
Something of God's
A gift from Him to us
Enormous snow cone shining bright
So full of beauty you have to climb it

---

*These sample poems were created by the sixth grade class of Betty Van Arsdale, East Lansdowne Elementary School, William Penn School District, Lansdowne, Pa.

CAMEO

People
In the darkness, still,
Watching for the sparkling fireworks
In a trance.
Firecrackers pop and snap loudly
A blare of light flashes and
Is gone.

CINQUAIN

Circus
Men on tight ropes
Many animal acts
Ladies on the flying trapeze
Jugglers

PENSEE

Phillies
Trying to win
Trying to beat every team
Playing to get the World Series
Playing the best they can.

TANKA

Softly the wind blows
It is is cool and breezy, too
The wind blows and whines
While the breeze remains silent
To birds it feels like winter.

LANTERNE

Help
Is there
When you need
To be rescued
Fast.

SEPTET

Kitty cats
Exquisitely soft
Nocturnal in their own way
They sleep in the day and play at night
Catnip attracts the kittens
Slowly they grow up
Then a cat.

Discussion

This center may lead children to an appreciation of poetry and literature in general. New poetry forms, such as concrete, diamante, septolet, and quinzaine, may be added to the center. For a good description of these poetry forms see *Contemporary English in the Elementary School* by Iris M. and Sidney W. Tiedt, Englewood Cliffs, N.J., Prentice-Hall, 1975, Chapter 8.

Some children may show an interest in more classic forms of poetry. Have lots of books available and schedule poetry readings of poems by class poets, as well as by known poets.

If children are enthusiastic about this center, it may lead you to add a variety of additional stations in related language arts topics. For example, you may create centers dealing with various figures of speech. You may also extend the work on syllabication by adding stations on stress and accent, pitch, and juncture.

If children become curious about Japanese art forms, you may create centers on calligraphy, the tea ceremony, flower arranging, and such. The students might be interested in other Japanese customs such as food or religion, and you may develop social studies centers on contemporary Japanese life as well as on aspects of Japanese history.

Language Derivatives

LEARNING CENTER NO. 10   LANGUAGE ARTS LEVELS 5-6

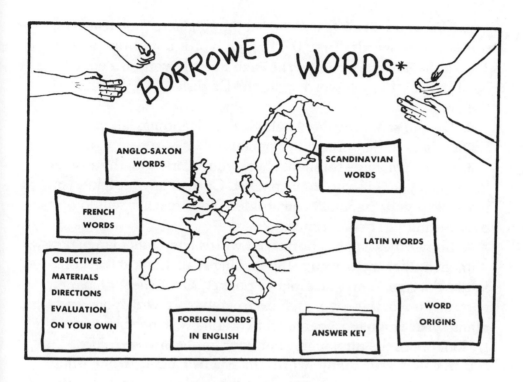

BORROWED WORDS

For the Student

Objective

You will discover that you can figure out many foreign words. You will learn that all languages borrow from each other, and therefore some words in English are similar to words in foreign languages.

You will trace the origin of some words.

---

*Developed from ideas contributed by Richard Bucciarelli.

Materials

You will need a pencil, paper, language reference books.

Directions

1. First you will try to guess what the English equivalent is for some foreign words. Take the French words out of the pocket. Take a sheet of paper and write each French word in a column. Next to each French word write the English word you think is the same.

2. Do the same for the Anglo-Saxon, Scandinavian, and the Latin words in the three other pockets.

3. When you have finished, check your work with the answer key which you will find in the pocket. Correct any mistakes you made. Put your paper in your folder. Your teacher will look it over during your conference.

4. Sometimes English borrowed words from other languages without bothering to change the spelling at all. Look at the words in the Foreign Words in English pocket. On a sheet of paper, copy any ten of these words. Next to each word write your guess about what language it came from originally. Check your work by looking in the dictionary. Put your paper in your folder.

5. As you see, many words in English came from other languages. Sometimes the spelling changed and sometimes the word remained the same. Sometimes the meaning changed somewhat, too. Tracing the origins of words can be very interesting. Look at the words in the Word Origins pocket. Use the dictionary or one of the language reference books at this center to trace the origin of any five (or more if you wish) of these words. Put your completed paper in your folder.

Evaluation

Check your own work for the tasks that are self-checking.

Your teacher will go over all your papers during your conference.

On Your Own

1. Frankfurters and hamburgers are favorite foods in America. What language did these words come from?

Make a list of all the foods that are very popular in America that have foreign names. Tell which country or language they come from.

2. Choose some common words, such as:

mother	hello	stop	please
father	goodbye	go	thanks

and try to find out how to say these words in other languages such as French, Spanish, German, Russian. Ask people who speak these languages, or look in foreign dictionaries.

3. Try to find the origin and meaning of your own name in one of the language reference sources at this center.

4. List some of the slang words you and your friends use today. See if you can trace their origin.

Can you identify the equivalent words or expressions used by your parents' generation for the same terms? Interview your parents or grandparents, or look in the slang dictionary.

Suggestions for the Teacher—Learning Center No. 10

Objectives

This center invites students to become linguists, to become engaged in the scholarly research of their own and foreign languages.

The study of the origin and history of language is in itself a fascinating subject for the middle grades. In addition, it is an excellent means of formal word study and vocabulary expansion. This center just introduces the broad topic of the history of language. It should be further developed through successive centers dealing with topics such as: how language first began, the history of the alphabet, growth and change in the English language, etc.

Directions for Making the Center

1. Use bright posterboard for the background.

2. Draw an appropriate theme, such as the map and hands depicted here, or a word tree.

3. Attach seven pockets or envelopes to the posterboard to hold the various sheets and cards the pupils will need to work with.

4. Choose ten words in French, ten in Scandinavian, ten in Anglo-Saxon, ten in Latin (or in any other languages) that have very similar equivalent words in English. Write each foreign word on an index card and put it in the appropriate pocket.

5. Make up an answer key for each foreign language. List the foreign word and its English counterpart. Examples are given.

Answer Key French Words	
ancien	ancient
bargaine	bargain
boeuf	beef
couleur	color
cri	cry
danse	dance
docteur	doctor
jardin	garden
miroir	mirror
montaigne	mountain

Answer Key Anglo-Saxon Words	
bedd	bed
beginan	begin
cradel	cradle
cuppe	cup
eorthe	earth
fyr	fire
glof	glove
middel	middle
singan	sing
slaepan	sleep

Answer Key Scandinavian Words			
hitta	hit	skinn	skin
hreindyri	reindeer	skraema	scream
illr	ill	skyrta	skirt
klubba	club	spikr	spike, nail
mugge	mug	theirra	their

Answer Key Latin Words			
factum	fact	pater	father
fascinare	fascinate	reducere	reduce
historia	history	relativus	relative
immediatus	immediate	separare	separate
opinio	opinion	totus	total

6. Make a list of about 20 foreign words that remained the same in English; or list each word separately on an index card. Put these words in the Foreign Words in English pocket. Examples are given.

Foreign Words in English				
beau	chateau	limousine	rodeo	adios
chartreuse	kid	bazaar	cognac	moose
samovar	soprano	pumpernickel	tattoo	alphabet
sampan	niche	chef	opera	moccasin
sky	toboggan	llama	status	chocolate

7. Make a list of words with interesting derivations; or write each word separately on an index card. Put these words in the Word Origins pocket. Examples are given.

Look Up the Origin		
pioneer	dandelion	vaseline
side burns	jeep	mustache
bazooka	money	candidate
bread	vaccinate	sacrifice
trivial	crinoline	mercy
chuckle	knickers	magpie

8. Laminate, or cover with clear plastic, all papers or cards that need to be preserved. Key all papers and cards so that they may easily be returned to the right pockets if they are misfiled.

Discussion

As Marshall McLuhan has pointed out, TV, Telstar, jets have turned the world into a global village. Our language quickly reflects this, with words travelling back and forth between different countries. Children need to realize the dynamics of our changing language, and to respect the contributions made to English by other languages. Inspiring children with a curiosity about words and with an interest in foreign languages expands their horizons.

If children show an interest in this subject there are many interesting projects that they can pursue. Looking up the origins and categories of surnames, learning how new words are coined, grouping languages into families and seeing how words cross borders, etc., are all good topics for learning-centered activities.

There should be an ample supply of dictionaries both in English and in other languages available at this center. There should also be on hand some of the fine books on linguistics and the history of words and language designed for elementary and high school students. Some titles are:

The First Book of Words by Samuel and Beryl Epstein
Thereby Hangs a Tale by Charles Funk
Word Origins and Their Romantic Stories by Wilfred Funk
Words, Things, and Celebrations by Wendell S. Johnson
Words Come In Families by Edward Horowitz

For a splendid list of such books see *Contemporary English in the Elementary School* by Iris M. Tiedt and Sidney W. Tiedt.

Numeration

LEARNING CENTER NO. 11   MATHEMATICS LEVELS K-1

GINGERBREAD MATH

For the Student

Objective

You will match a gingerbread man who has a numeral on him with a gingerbread man who has the same number of raisins on him.

Materials

You will need a pencil, scissors, brown construction paper, crayons, paste.

---

*Developed from ideas contributed by Cathy Weibly.

Directions

1. Take a gingerbread man from the pocket.

2. Count the raisins on the gingerbread man.

3. Find the gingerbread man on the board who has the numeral that matches the number of raisins. Stick your gingerbread man on top of him.

4. Do the same with all the other gingerbread men in the pocket.

Evaluation

1. Turn each raisin gingerbread man over. Look at the numeral on the back. See if the numeral on the back of the raisin gingerbread man is the same as the numeral on the gingerbread man you matched it with.

2. Did you get all of them right? Fill out the score sheet. Put it in the basket.

3. Put the raisin gingerbread men back in the pocket.

On Your Own

1. Take a sheet of construction paper. Take the gingerbread pattern from the pocket. Use the pattern to trace some gingerbread men. Cut them out.

2. Paste raisins on your gingerbread men.

3. On the back of each gingerbread man you made, write the numeral that tells how many raisins you pasted on him. You may color your gingerbread men. After you show them to your teacher, you may take them home.

4. If you would like, make up a new center by yourself. You may draw any form you like—balls, cars, snowmen, etc. Draw them on the construction paper. Then put numerals on them. Then cut out forms exactly like the ones you drew. Paste raisins, or pebbles, or buttons, or anything else you can think of on your cut-outs. Be sure to write the correct numeral on the back of each cut-out. Show your work to your teacher.

Gingerbread Math Score Sheet

_____   _____
                Name   *Date*

I got _____ right.

I got _____ wrong.

Suggestions for the Teacher—Learning Center No. 11

Objectives

Matching an abstract numeral with a concrete number (set) of objects is an important beginning skill in mathematics. This center involves the child in an imaginative activity which promotes this skill. It also provides practice in the much needed perceptual and manipulative skills of matching, tracing, cutting, pasting.

This center also introduces children to learning centers at an early age. The activity is simple enough so that children may engage in it independently or in pairs, learning the procedures involved in working in a learning center.

Directions for Making the Center

1. On a posterboard, draw a dog (or another animal) with a chef's hat and a rolling pin. Draw 11 gingerbread men within a dough-like shape. On each gingerbread man print a numeral from 0 to 10.

2. Draw and cut out 11 more gingerbread men exactly like the others. Paste from 0 to 10 raisins on each gingerbread man. Print the appropriate numerals on the backs of the gingerbread men so that the center is self-checking.

3. Put adhesive or velcro strips on the gingerbread men so that the children can stick them together when they match them.

4. Run off Score Sheets. Put them in the Directions pocket.

5. Mount a pocket or envelope to store the gingerbread men.

6. Make a gingerbread man pattern out of oaktag to be used by the children for the On Your Own activity. Put it in a pocket on the posterboard.

7. Provide a box of raisins.

8. Have all the other needed supplies available (scissors, paste, construction paper).

Discussion

An excellent preparatory activity to lead into this center is the actual baking of gingerbread men using a cooky cutter and putting on raisin faces and buttons.

This center should be used early in the year. The mathematical concept is appropriate for young children. It is also an excellent introduction to the learning center. The teacher should explain and guide children in the procedures and use of the learning center, explaining how to work independently, how to check your own work, and how to create new materials of your own.

Addition and Subtraction

LEARNING CENTER NO. 12   MATHEMATICS LEVELS 1-2

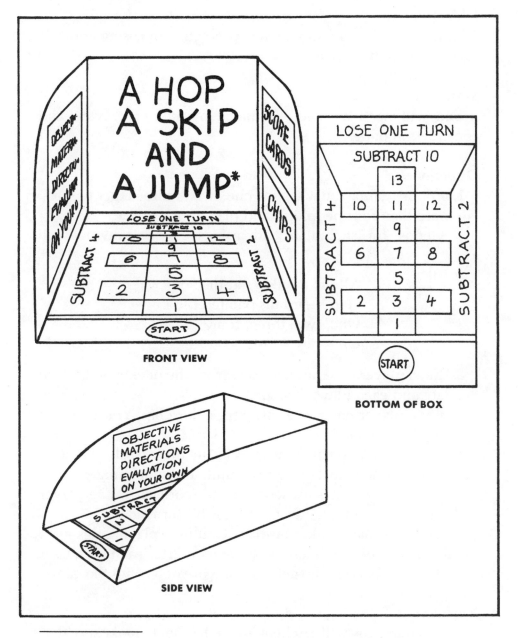

FRONT VIEW

BOTTOM OF BOX

SIDE VIEW

---

*Developed from ideas contributed by James MacCall and Marianne Straub.

A HOP, A SKIP, AND A JUMP

For the Student

Objective

At this center you will play a hopscotch game using addition and subtraction.

Materials

You will need a pencil, a magic marker or crayon, and construction paper.

Directions

1. For this game you will need one, two or three other players. No more than four people should play at one time.

2. Choose for 1st, 2nd, 3rd, 4th, using a choosing rhyme, such as:

> All the monkeys at the zoo
> Had their tails painted blue.
> One, two, three, four,
> Out goes Y-O-U.

3. Each player takes a score card from the pocket and fills in the date and each player's name.

4. Each player chooses a different color chip. You will find them in the envelope.

5. The first player puts his chip in the Start circle. Then he flips it down the board using his thumb and index finger.

6. Everybody writes his score on the score card. The player picks up his chip and holds it until it is his turn again.

7. The next player takes his turn. Continue playing this way. Total everybody's score on the score card after each round.

8. The first player who gets a total score of 50 wins the game.

Evaluation

As you play, you will be checking each other to make sure that you are all keeping score correctly. If there is a disagreement, ask someone in the room to check you out.

Put all the completed score cards back in the pocket for your teacher to check. Put your initials under your total score.

On Your Own

Try to design a different playing board for this game. You can use different shapes, and put your numbers wherever you want. Draw your game board on a sheet of construction paper. When you are finished, show it to your teacher. He will help you put it on posterboard for a new center.

Suggestions for the Teacher—Learning Center No. 12

Objectives

Especially at the early beginnings, but also later on, just plain practice and drill are needed for reinforcing skills in computation, which depend primarily on memory. Using flash cards and workbooks can be boring. Games, on the other hand, lend themselves beautifully to math skill building and are highly motivational. In a game, as in life, the computations are the means and not the end.

The board game presented here uses the simplest format for beginners in math.

Directions for Making the Center

1. This center is mounted in a box with three standing sides. Cut away the front of the box and round off the sides.

2. Draw the hopscotch diagram on the bottom of the box.

3. Tack a pocket or envelope to one side for the directions.

4. Run off a batch of Score Sheets and put them in a pocket on the other side of the box. (See sample.)

5. Attach an envelope with four different colored chips to the side of the box. (Poker or backgammon chips are good.)

Discussion

This center is easily adapted to other levels. If you make the gameboard on a separate piece of cardboard and lay it on the bottom of the box, it may easily be changed as the children's skills advance. The numbers may be changed; the directions may be made more complex; fractions may be included, etc.

This is only one game format, and a very simple one. Many other board games may be created using bowling, shuffleboard and other themes.

A Hop, A Skip, and A Jump **Score Card** _____ *Date*			
ROUND	**PLAYERS' NAMES**		
1			
2			
Total			
3			
Total			
4			
Total			
5			
Total			
TOTAL			

Also, card and dice games offer many opportunities for the practice of math skills at every level. The teacher will find that some games, such as Casino and 500 Rummy, may be used in their original form, and that other games are easily adaptable for school use. An excellent book with many game ideas is Herbert Kohl's *Math, Writing & Games in the Open Classroom*. Another book with many games for classroom use is *Deal Me In! A Guide to the Use of Card Games As Learning Tools* by Margie Golick.

Addition of Money

LEARNING CENTER NO. 13   MATHEMATICS LEVELS 1-2

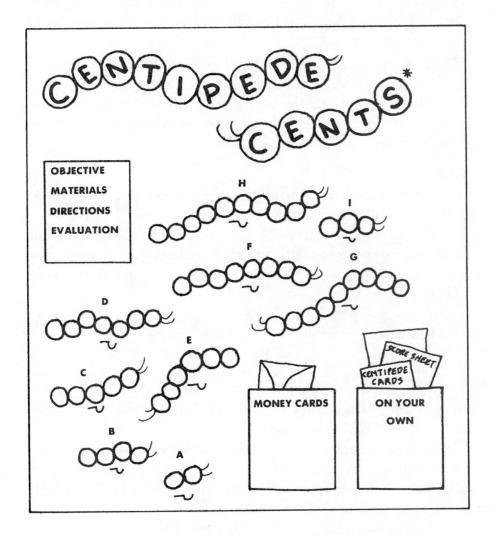

Objective

At this center you will count how many cents different centipedes are worth.

---

*Developed from ideas contributed by Pat Carlisle.

Materials

You will need a pencil, and a magic marker or felt pen.

Directions

1. Take one of the cards from the Money Cards pocket. Read the amount on it.

2. Find the centipede that matches the card—it has the same amount of cents as the total on the card.

3. Hang the card on the hook under this centipede.

4. Do the rest of the cards in the same way. Sometimes you will put more than one card on a hook.

Evaluation

When you have hung up all the cards, check your own work. Take a Score Sheet from the pocket.

Take one card off the hook. Turn it over. If the letter on the back is the same as the letter over the centipede, you were right. Check the score sheet. (Sometimes you will have more than one check in a box.)

Do the same with all the cards.

When you have finished, put your score sheet in the basket.

On Your Own

1. Pick a centipede card from the On Your Own folder. Add up the value of the centipede. Write the total number of cents on the On Your Own Score Sheet.

Now take enough coins from the envelope to make this exact amount of money. Draw the coins on the score sheet. Put the coins back in the envelope. Check your work by looking at the answers on the back of the centipede card.

2. Do the same for all the centipede cards.

3. Take a blank card from the pocket. Draw your own centipede with a magic marker or a felt pen. Be sure to put the total value of your centipede on the back of the card. Draw the coins for this amount of money on the back of the card. Show your teacher your card. He may put it in the On Your Own pocket for your friends to do.

Centipede Cents
Score Sheet

*Name*_____   *Date*_____

	Right	Wrong
A		
B		
C		
D		
E		
F		
G		
H		
I		
Total		

Centipede Cents
On Your Own Score Sheet

*Name*_____   *Date*_____

Card No.	Total Amount	Coins	Right	Wrong
1				
2				
3				
4				
5				

Suggestions for the Teacher—Learning Center No. 13

Objective

Teaching children to count money can begin at an early age.

This center provides children with a simple activity counting coins at a very elementary level. We begin by simply totalling pennies. Recognizing how many cents are equivalent to a nickel and to a dime is a next step. For children who are more advanced, more complicated tasks in counting money and matching these totals with their coin values are provided.

Directions for Making the Center

1. Mount this center on a colorful posterboard. You will find pictures of pennies in math workbooks. Glue these to the poster-board to form the nine centipede bodies with values from 2¢ to 10¢.

2. Above each centipede place a letter. Below each centipede place a drapery hook.

3. Mount three pockets on the posterboard—for the directions, for the Money Cards, and for the On Your Own tasks.

4. Using index cards, make 15 Money Cards representing values from 2¢-10¢. The first nine cards will just have the totals from 2¢ to 10¢ on them. The next four cards will have a picture of a nickel, plus the appropriate number of cents. One card will have pictures of two nickels, and one card will have a picture of a dime.

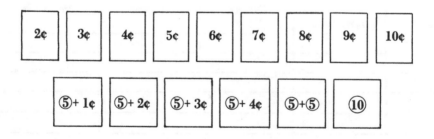

5. On the back of each money card write the letter of the centipede it matches.

6. Make five centipede cards for the On Your Own tasks. Make them as easy or as difficult as is appropriate for your children. Examples are given. Number each card and put the

answers, including the total amount of money and pictures of the coins totalling this amount, on the back of each card.

7. Put four pennies, a nickel and a number of dimes in an envelope in the On Your Own pocket.

8. Put some blank index cards in the On Your Own pocket.

9. Run off Score Sheets. Put them in the Directions pocket.

10. Run off On Your Own Score Sheets. Put them in the On Your Own pocket.

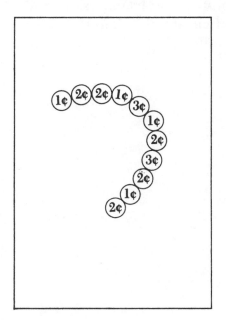 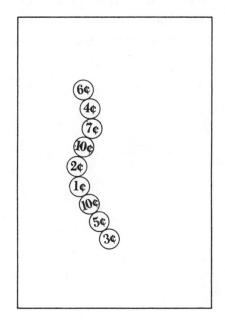

Discussion

This center can be constantly expanded by changing the centipede pictures to include coins of all denominations, and increasing the value of the money cards. Eventually, sophisticated money calculations involving dollars and cents may be provided. This progression should, of course, keep pace with the actual progress of the children. This center may be one that is designed for only part of the class. Later on, these children may help the others as they become ready.

Real and simulated money experiences should be an integral part of the primary curriculum. Going to the store to buy ingredients for a cooking activity, or to buy needed school supplies gives children a real understanding of money transactions.

Setting up a classroom store with empty containers of all kinds, using real or play money, is in itself an important learning center.

Other real experiences with money can be planned on a simple level—baking and selling cookies, conducting a flea market with old books and toys, etc. The teacher should also encourage parents to give children simple chores involving money—buying the newspaper, milk, a loaf of bread, etc.

Mathematics Concepts

LEARNING CENTER NO. 14   MATHEMATICS LEVELS 3-4

500 MILE RACE*

OBJECTIVE

MATERIALS

DIRECTIONS

EVALUATION

ON YOUR OWN

*Developed from ideas contributed by Janice Arnold.

500 MILE RACE

For the Student

Objective

At this center you will play a game using dice that will give you practice with various math skills.

Materials

You will need a pencil and paper.

Directions

1. You may play this game by yourself, or with one, two, or three other players. Each player completes his own Individual Score Sheet, and also enters his score on the Group Tally Sheet.

2. If you are playing alone, roll the three dice and record your roll on the Individual Score Sheet—enter the number on each die, the sum of the three dice, and write Yes or No to indicate whether you achieved the objective for the mileage. If you wrote No, keep rolling and recording the results.

3. When you succeed, enter on the Group Tally Sheet the total number of rolls you made in order to achieve that objective.

4. Then go on to the next mileage marker. Follow the same procedure, recording each roll on the Individual Score Sheet, and the sum of the rolls needed to reach each mileage objective on the Group Tally Sheet.

5. When you have completed the 500 Mile Race, total all your rolls and enter this score on the Class Score Sheet. When everybody in the class has completed this game, we will rank each player.

6. If you are playing with other players, each player takes only one turn rolling at a time. He records his results and waits for his next turn to roll again. If he was successful, he will go on to the next mileage objective on his next turn. If he was not successful, he will try again on his next turn.

7. Whenever someone wins the game, he may go on to another center. The other players continue playing, rolling and

recording their results, until each player has reached the final destination. As each player completes the game, he writes his name and total score on the Class Score Sheet.

Evaluation

1. Put your Individual Score Sheet in your folder. Your teacher will check it with you during your conference.

2. If two, three or four students are playing together, they check each others' work as the game progresses.

On Your Own

1. Create a new Group Tally Sheet. Take a different route. Look in the Atlas and choose cities along the route. Write down the mileage from the first city to each successive city.

2. Write new directions for each mileage marker you have chosen.

3. You might want to use a different theme—golf, tennis, basketball, etc. Make up an appropriate Group Tally Sheet.

Suggestions for the Teacher—Learning Center No. 14

Objectives

Many times the review or reinforcement of math skills becomes a boring chore. This center provides practice in those skills in a different and interesting manner. Hopefully this format enables students to become so involved with playing, that the use of math skills becomes a challenge intrinsic to the game.

Directions for Making the Learning Center

1. This entire center can be housed in an 8½" x 11" manila envelope. The Objective, Directions, Evaluation, On Your Own can be made into a small booklet stapled to the outside of the envelope.

2. Make up a Group Tally Sheet. Use actual cities and actual mileages.

500 Mile Race

Group Tally Sheet

DESTINATION	MILE-AGE	PLAYERS' NAMES			OBJECTIVE
New York City	0	*Record total number of rolls needed to reach each city's objective.*			
Trenton, N.J.	62				1. Roll a total sum which is an odd number.
Phila., Pa.	91				2. Roll a total sum that is more than 6, but less than 12.
Wilmington, Del.	117				3. Roll a total sum that can be divided by 3 with no remainder.
Baltimore, Md.	187				4. Roll a total sum that is a multiple of 5.
Washington, D.C.	225				5. Roll a total sum that is less than 7.
Fredericksburg, Va.	281				6. Roll a total sum that is a prime number.
Richmond, Va.	340				7. Roll a total sum of 13.
Newport News, Va.	402				8. Roll a total that is an even number greater than 8.
Elizabeth City, N. C.	467				9. Roll a total that is an odd number greater than 9.
Cape Hatteras N. C.	569				10. Roll a product (of 2 or 3 dice) that is a prime number.
Total Number of Rolls					*The winner is_____*

500 Mile Race Individual Score Sheet			
Name		Date	
Roll No.	Numbers On Each Die	Total	Was Objective Achieved?
1			
2			
3			
4			
5			
6			
7			
8			
9			
10			
11			
12			
13			
14			
15			

500 Mile Race Class Score Sheet		
NAME	Total Score	Rank

3. Make up objectives for the Group Tally Sheet that give students practice in math concepts taught.

4. Run off enough Individual Score Sheets and Group Tally Sheets for the class.

5. Only one Class Score Sheet is needed. The students will write in their own names. Ranking will take place when everybody has finished the game.

6. Be sure to include three dice in the envelope.

Discussion

This game is adaptable to any grade level. The objectives will be based on the skills and concepts for which practice is needed. Those given here are samples.

If the game is popular, the objectives may be revised and the game continued.

If a student creates his own game, he may supervise the players and check their work.

Estimating

LEARNING CENTER NO. 15   MATHEMATICS LEVELS 4-6

*Developed from ideas contributed by James MacCall and Marianne Straub.

WHAT'S YOUR GUESS

For the Student

Objective

Did you ever go to a carnival or fair and see a showman who promises to guess your weight within a pound? Did you ever ask the butcher for 1½ lbs. of steak and watch him cut it exactly? These skills come from practice and experience.

At this center you will practice making estimates about the size, quantity, weight of different things, as well as about time and money.

Materials

You will need: a ruler, pencil, writing paper, toy catalog, newspaper, stopwatch, clock.

Directions

1. Find a partner. Each take an Estimating Sheet from the pocket.

2. Look at the items on the table. Beside each item is a card with directions. Pick any one item together.

3. Each of you make your own estimate following the directions on the card. Record your answer on your Estimating Sheet. Compare and discuss your answers together.

4. Now check your answers by counting, measuring, or weighing the item as directed. Record the result on your Estimating Sheet. Compare your estimate with the actual answer. How close were you?

5. When you have finished this first item, pick another one. Continue in the same way until you have done all the items on the table.

6. Try to improve on your estimates as you go along by using your experience and by careful observation.

7. Do the On Your Own activities together.

8. Put your finished Estimating Sheets in your folder to be seen by your teacher.

Evaluation

You will check your own answers by counting, measuring, or weighing each item with your partner.

On Your Own

With your partner, do as many of the activities on these cards as you like. Be sure to record your estimates and then the answer you got by exact measurement.

1. *Quantity, Volume*
   a. Find a classroom window from which you can see children on the playground. Estimate the number you see; write it down; then count the children; write down the actual number. Were you right?
   b. Go to the library. Select any one shelf of books. Estimate the number of books on it; then count them.
   c. Get an empty coffee can. Estimate the number of cups of water it will take to fill it; then count the cups as you fill it.

2. *Length*
   a. Estimate the length of your classroom. Then get a yardstick and measure it.
   b. Select the tallest child in your class. Estimate his height; then measure him.
   c. Estimate the length of the longest table in your classroom. Then get a ruler and measure it.

3. *Weight*
   a. Select two children in your class who look as though they are the same weight. Estimate their weight and then weigh them to see how close you came.
   b. Select a chair in the classroom. Estimate its weight; then weigh it. (Problem: How do you weigh a chair?)
   c. Select a dictionary and an encyclopedia from your classroom. Estimate the difference between their weights; then weigh them to find the actual difference.

4. *Money*

a. Make a list of six toys or games you would like to have. Estimate the cost of each and their total cost. Look in a toy catalog or newspaper advertisement. Find the actual cost of each toy or game and their total cost.

b. Estimate how much money each of these things would cost: a 19-inch TV set, a Volkswagen, a 64-oz. bottle of Coca Cola. Then look in newspapers and magazines for advertisements. Write down the cheapest and the most expensive prices you find for each item. Did your estimates fall within these actual prices?

c. You get an allowance of a dollar a week. You want to buy a pair of roller skates which cost $6.39. You will pay for them with money you save out of your allowance. Estimate how many weeks it will take if you save 40¢ a week; 50¢ a week; 60¢ a week. Then figure how many weeks it will actually take you if you save these different amounts each week.

5. *Time*

a. Select a book you think you will enjoy reading. Estimate how many pages you can read in 15 minutes. Time yourself with a timer or get someone to time you. Read at your normal speed. See how many pages you actually read.

b. If you were to call a friend and he doesn't answer right away, how many rings do you think you would hear if you listened for one minute before hanging up? Write down your estimate. Then call someone you know is not at home (your teacher for example). Time yourself and listen for one minute, counting the rings.

c. Sit in a place where you can see a clock or a watch with a second hand. When the second hand reaches 12, close your eyes. Keep them closed until you think 30 seconds have passed. Open your eyes and check how right or wrong you were. Do this several times until your accuracy improves.

6. Make up a set of estimating problems. Find another pair

who have worked at this center. Exchange problems—you do the ones they made up and give them yours.

Suggestions for the Teacher—Learning Center No. 15

Objectives

The skill of estimating is a practical one that is used throughout one's life. For example, we all have to estimate the time needed to get a job done, and how much money is needed to buy food. Children need practice in learning this skill. This center provides practice in estimating through a series of stimulating experiences using very ordinary items. The center is made more inviting by having some of the items edible.

Directions for Making the Center

1. Set this center up on a table, backed by a wall or bulletin board on which the name of the center and pockets for Directions and Estimating Sheets can be placed.

2. Arrange the items to be estimated on the table. Write or type the directions for each item on a card, folded into an inverted V-shape. Set it beside the item.

3. Make up an Estimating Sheet and place copies in the pocket. (Example is given.) No answer sheet is necessary because children prove the correct answers for each item by actually counting, measuring, or weighing and by verifying their answers with each other.

ESTIMATING SHEET

Name _____   *Date* _____

MACARONI	SODA BOTTLE CAP	SAND
Estimate _____ pcs.	Estimate _____ drops	Estimate _____ tb.
Actual _____ pcs.	Actual _____ drops	Actual _____ tb.

4. Make certain to have rulers, yardsticks, scales, and a stop watch available.

5. In the sketch for this center, some of the items that should be placed on the table have been omitted, only because there is not enough room to draw them all. All the materials suggested for the center, however, should be placed on the table.

6. Make up cards for the On Your Own activities.

Suggested Estimating Problems:

NUMBER AND VOLUME

MACARONI

1. How many pieces are in the jar?

2. Record your estimate.

3. Open the jar and count them.

4. Record your answer.

SODA BOTTLE CAP

1. How many drops of water will it take to fill the soda bottle cap?

2. Record your estimate.

3. Put water in the cup. Fill the eyedropper with water from the cup. Now slowly fill the soda bottle cap and count the number of drops. Stop when the bottle cap first runs over.

4. Record your answer.

SAND

1. How many tablespoons of sand will it take to fill the cup?

2. Record your estimate.

3. Count the number of tablespoonsfuls needed. Level off each tablespoon of sand with the knife so they will all be the same size. Fill the cup level.

4. Record your answer.

LENGTH

PRETZEL STICK

1. Take out one of the pretzel sticks. How many inches long do you think it is?

2. Record your estimate.

3. Using the ruler, measure its actual length.

4. Record your answer.

5. Bite a piece off one end of the pretzel.

6. Estimate the remaining length.

7. Record your answer.

8. Measure it with a ruler.

9. Record your answer.

10. Eat the rest of the pretzel.

DRY SPAGHETTI

1. Take out one of the sticks of dry spaghetti. Be careful not to break it. How many inches long do you think it is?

2. Record you estimate.

3. Using the ruler, measure its actual length.

4. Record your answer.

DRINKING STRAWS

1. Pick out a drinking straw. Estimate its length in inches.

2. Record your estimate.

3. Using the ruler, measure its actual length.

4. Record your answer.

5. Use the scissors to cut off a small piece from each end. Estimate the length of the remaining piece.

6. Record your estimate.

7. Measure the actual length.

8. Record your answer.

CRACKERS

1. Take out one of the crackers. How long and how wide do you think it is?

2. Record your estimates to the nearest quarter inch.

3. Measure the cracker.

4. Record your answers.

5. Eat your cracker.

6. If every pupil in the class were to eat two crackers, how many boxes of crackers would be needed at this center?

7. Record your estimate.

8. Count the number of crackers in a box and the number of pupils in the room. Figure out the actual number of boxes of crackers needed.

9. Record your answer.

WEIGHT

BOOKS

1. Pick up each of the three books, one at a time. Which do you think is heaviest, and which is lightest? (Note: Provide books of varying sizes.)

2. Record your estimates.

3. Weigh the books.

4. Record your answers.

BALLS

1. Pick up the three balls, one at a time. Guess which ball is the heaviest and which is lightest.

2. Record your estimates.

3. Weigh the balls.

4. Record your answers.

TUBES

1. Pick up the four tubes, one at a time. Which is heaviest, which is lightest and which two weigh the same?

2. Record your estimates.

3. Weigh each tube.

4. Record your answers.

   Note: Provide four opaque tubes (or use cans) of equal size. Label A, B, C, D. Fill A with sand, B and C with dry cereals, and D with cotton.

TIME

ERASING CHALKBOARD

1. How long do you think it will take you to erase one section of the chalkboard?

2. Record your estimate.

3. Have your partner write, draw or scribble all over the section.

4. Erase the board while your partner times you using the stop watch.

5. Record the actual time it took you.

COPYING

1. Choose a page or a paragraph from one of your reading, science, social studies textbooks or from

a library book. How long do you think it will take you to copy it?

2. Record your estimate.

3. Turn on the stop watch. Copy the selection. Turn off the stop watch.

4. Record the actual time it took you.

WALKING

1. Have you ever stopped to think how long it takes you to walk from one place to another? Go to the end of the hallway outside your room. How long do you think it will take you to walk to the other end and back using a normal pace—no running?

2. Record your estimate.

3. Turn on the stop watch. Walk to the other end and back. Turn off the stop watch.

4. Record the actual time it took you.

MONEY

GROCERY ITEMS

1. Look at the grocery store items on the table. How much do you think each one costs?

2. Record your estimates.

3. Look on the bottom of each item for the actual cost.

4. Compare the actual cost with your estimated amounts.

    Note to teacher: Provide ordinary items such as a box of cookies, bottle of soda, (empty) milk container, can of tuna, box of cereal, etc.

SCHOOL SUPPLIES

1. You use school supplies in the classroom all the time. Did you ever wonder how much they cost? Look at the items on the table. How much do you think the school had to pay for each one?

2. Record your estimates.

3. Check for the correct answers on the back of this direction card.

4. Record your answers.

    Note to teacher: Provide frequently used classroom items such as chalkboard eraser, dictionary, jar of paste, scissors, ruler, box of chalk, etc. Write the costs of each on the back of the directions card.

CLEAN UP

1. Have you ever thought about how much the items you use for washing up and getting ready for school cost? Look at these items on the table. How much do you think each of these costs?

2. Record your estimates.

3. Look on the bottom of each article to find its actual cost.

4. Compare the actual prices with your estimates.

5. If all these items were to last for 30 days, what do you think it costs on the average to wash up and get ready for school each day?

6. Record your estimate.

7. Figure out how much it would actually cost per day.

Note to teacher: Provide empty containers of soap, toothpaste, shampoo, toothbrush, and facial tissue. Write the price on the bottom of each container.

Discussion

This center is directly experiential and can be used to introduce a unit on estimating, or it can be used for enrichment of the study of estimating.

Practice in metric measurements could be given by asking for answers in metrics, or in both metrics and English units for weight and length.

The center could be changed and continued simply by adding new activities. It could be increased in difficulty by adding more complex estimating tasks.

An excellent subsidiary class activity is conducting a contest estimating the number of pieces of candy or pennies in a jar. This contest could run for three weeks and include other classes. Children could submit their first estimates on a form provided during the first week. They can then be given the opportunity to revise their estimates the day before the count takes place. The three persons making the closest estimates might divide the contents of the jar.

Mathematical Operations

LEARNING CENTER NO. 16   MATHEMATICS LEVELS 5-7

DINING OUT

For the Student

Objective

At this center you will dine at different restaurants and select items from menus, using the basic mathematical operations.

Materials

You will need pen or pencil and writing paper.

Directions

1. Choose any one of the activity cards.
2. Find a menu in the pocket that goes with the activity card you selected.

---

*Developed from ideas contributed by James MacCall and Marianne Straub.

3. Take a Dining Out answer sheet from the basket. Write your name and the date at the top.

4. Complete the activities on your card. Enter your answers on the answer sheet. (You may use the back of the answer sheet for your calculations.)

5. Look at the back of the activity card to see if the answers are given. If they are, check your work.

6. Continue in the same manner until you have completed all the activity cards.

7. Put your completed answer sheet back in the basket.

Evaluation

1. If you have a card that has fixed answers, you will find them on the back of the activity card.

2. If the activity card has the name of a student who made it up, show your work to him.

3. You may ask one of the class Math Whiz Kids to check you out if you like.

4. Your teacher will discuss your work with you during your conference.

On Your Own

Make up your own activity card using any menu. Show your idea to your teacher. He will tell you whether to add your activity card to the center for others to do.

Suggestions for the Teacher—Learning Center No. 16

Objectives

Most children enjoy poring over contemporary catalogs, ads, and menus and making selections. This center provides practical experience in using math in life-like situations.

It also encourages a degree of social competence and sophistication in a familiar area of life-experience—eating out. Becoming knowledgeable about all kinds of menu items (common, ethnic, gourmet), and about restaurant terms and procedures is a social grace pre-adolescents enjoy cultivating.

Directions for Making the Learning Center

1. Collect menus from various restaurants, or make up your own menus. Try to include various cuisines—French, Italian, Seafood, American, Chinese.

2. On a sheet of oaktag or cardboard, create a simple restaurant scene.

3. Attach a pocket to hold the menus, and one to hold the activity cards.

4. Based on the menus, make up activity cards. Samples are given below.

5. Put the answers on the backs of those cards that have fixed answers.

6. Provide a basket for Dining Out answer sheets. Check this basket periodically, removing the completed sheets and checking them with the students.

Activity Card 1

1. You have won a contest sponsored by Antoine's Restaurant. Your prize is one of each dessert listed on the menu. How much money is your prize worth?

2. In addition to you, there were 22 other winners in the contest. How much did the contest cost the restaurant?

3. How would you use up your prize—one dessert a day? two a day? invite a friend? Any other ideas?

4. Which of the desserts is your favorite? If you could have your favorite dessert over and over again instead of a different dessert each time, would it cost the restaurant more or less?

Activity Card 2

You have invited seven friends to celebrate your birthday with you. Your parents have given you the choice of having a pizza and coke party at home for your friends, or taking them all to a hamburger joint.

1. Look at the take-out pizza menu. Figure that you'll have to have two or three slices per kid. Figure that each kid will have between 12 and 16 ounces of coke. How much would the party at home cost?

2. Look at the Hamburger Heaven menu. Figure each kid will have two hamburgers and a large coke. How much would it cost to eat out?

3. Which will you choose to do?

Activity Card 3

1. Decide what kind of food you are in the mood for—Italian, French, Chinese, American. Find the appropriate menu.

2. Choose a complete dinner from the menu. A complete dinner includes: appetizer, soup, entrée, dessert, and beverage. List your choices for each of these courses.

3. How much does your dinner cost?

4. If you were with two other people who ordered the same dinner, how much would the total bill be?

5. It is customary to leave a 15% tip for the waiter. How much would you leave for the three of you (round off your figure)?

Activity Card 4

You and your parents are spending the summer at the shore. One night, your mother announces that she is tired of cooking, so Dad takes you out to a fancy seafood restaurant.

This is what you order:

DAD:	Oysters Rockefeller	MOM:	Clam chowder
	Broiled lobster		Fresh boneless shad
	Cheesecake		Mint parfait
	Coffee		Coffee

YOU: Shrimp cocktail
        Seafood combination platter
        Pie à la mode
        Coca cola

1. Whose dinner was the most expensive?
2. Whose was the least expensive?
3. Each of you ordered à la carte, but there was a table d'hôte menu that had a prix-fixe of $10.95. If each of you had ordered the prix-fixe dinner, how much money would Dad have saved?

Activity Card 5

1. You and your friend are in the mood for Chinese food, but you have only $10.00 between you. What could you order? List your choices and the cost of each.
2. Do you have any money left for a tip? How much could you leave? If the usual tip is 15%, would you have enough?

Activity Card 6

You have found a lost dog in your neighborhood and you return it to the owner. Your reward is a free dinner once a month for one year at Mother Bell's restaurant.

1. You love southern fried chicken, and order it each time. How much will this entrée cost for one year?
2. You also order Bavarian cream pie and milk every time. How much will this cost for one year?
3. How much was your reward worth?
4. If you had picked the most expensive entrée on the menu and ordered this each month, how much more would the reward have been worth?

Activity Card 7

For Father's Day, your grandfather sent your family a restaurant gift certificate. It is worth $70.00. Grandfather's instructions are that your family of six is to spend this money eating one meal together in any restaurant you choose.

1. Choose any menu you like. Find your favorite meat entrée on this menu. How much would it cost if all six of you had this entrée?

2. Now choose your favorite dessert. How much would it cost if all six of you had this dessert?

3. How much is left from the $70.00 now?

4. Look at the list of appetizers. Is there enough money left to pay for six appetizers if you all had the same one? Would there be enough money for each of the six of you to choose any appetizer you wanted?

Activity Card 8

1. Using the menu for Charles' Continental Restaurant, add up the total cost of all the meat entrées.

2. Find the average cost of a meat entrée.

3. Add up the total cost of all the seafood entrées.

4. Find the average cost of a seafood entrée.

5. Is the average cost of a meat entrée higher or lower than the average cost of a seafood entrée?

Activity Card 9

1. Your father wants to make a big impression on someone by giving him the best meal in the most expensive restaurant in town. Glance through all the menus and pick out the restaurant that seems to be the most expensive.

2. Choose the most expensive appetizer, the most expensive entrée, and the most expensive dessert. Record your choices, and the cost of two of each.

3. Select the most expensive champagne on the menu.

4. How much change would your father receive from $100.00?

Activity Card 10

You love Italian food and enjoy everything on the menu. You are going to indulge yourself by eating in your favorite Italian restaurant every day for a week, choosing something different each day.

1. List the appetizers you would choose each day. What would the total cost of the appetizers be for a week? What would the average cost be?

2. List all the entrées you would eat during the week. What would the total cost be? What would the average cost be?

3. What would the average cost of both an appetizer and entrée be for one day?

Discussion

This center assumes that the children have had experiences eating out and have a fairly advanced knowledge of the relevant vocabulary. It would be worth while for the teacher to introduce some preliminary class activities that would indicate the extent of the students' experiences and information.

Eating and cooking activities are marvelous sources of vocabulary and language work, as well as of math work. They are highly motivated and can be directly experiential if the teacher can plan some real shopping and cooking activities.

Studying about various ethnic food styles and customs is both interesting and educational. It gives students an appreciation and tolerance for the rich variation available and typical in the American style of life.

This center is easily adaptable to fit any area in the classroom. It is also very easily changed or renewed by changing the menus as well as the activity cards.

The center can also be varied by using mail order catalogs with items of furniture, clothing, toys, etc. Newspaper ads are another source for activity cards using mathematical operations.

The teacher might post lists of the names of students who are outstanding in various curricular areas. Students may use the math whiz kid to help them check their work at this center.

Mental Measurements

LEARNING CENTER NO. 17   MATHEMATICS LEVELS 5-6

MATH GYMNASTICS

For the Student

Objective

You will solve math problems by doing mental arithmetic. You will use addition, subtraction, multiplication, and division with liquid, length, time, and counting measurements. You will use English and metric units.

Materials

You will need a pencil, stop watch or clock.

Directions

1. There are four puzzle pockets on the center. Each contains 16 problems. You will work out all these problems in your head without using a pencil or paper. Before you start each puzzle, estimate how long you think it will take you to complete the 16 problems. This is your goal time.

2. Take an Answer Form from the pocket. Write your name, the date, and the number of the puzzle at the top. Write your goal time at the top—how many minutes you think it will take to do all the problems in Puzzle 1.

3. Take the cards out of the Puzzle 1 pocket. Each card has a math problem on it. Each card also has a letter and a number in the corner that matches a square on the Answer Form.

4. Record the time you start the first problem. Use a stop watch or clock to time yourself.

5. Take each card one at a time. Read the problem. Figure out the answer in your head without using a pencil. (This is called mental math.) Write the answer in the matching square on the Answer Form.

6. Do all 16 cards in this way. Remember—use mental math only. You may only use your pencil to write the answer.

7. When you have completed all 16 problems, record the time and the total actual time you spent.

8. To check your work:

a. Add all the numbers in the M column and write the total in the box at the bottom of the column. Do the same with the A, T, and H numbers.

b. Get the Puzzle Checker card for Puzzle 1 from the pocket. Use the card to check your work.

c. If your totals differ from the answers, try to find your mistake. If you are unable to find your error, ask one of your classmates for help. Or, ask your teacher for the Answer Check Sheet.

9. Follow the same procedure for the other three puzzles.

Evaluation

You will check your answers with the Puzzle Checker.

On Your Own

1. Make up any kind of math problems that will fit these answers. Your problems do not have to be about measurements only. For example: What is 18 less than 42?

M	A	T	H
12	24	8	7
46	9	2	36
14	18	60	90
52	3	4	15

2. Make up a new math puzzle by writing 16 problems using any measurements that you have worked on. Give your puzzle to

a classmate. Make up a Puzzle Checker. Give it to him when he finishes your puzzle.

Suggestions for the Teacher—Learning Center No. 17

Objectives

Children often do computations mechanically, relying on pencil and paper for even the most simple problems. The ability to do mental math problems is a critical skill and helps children to really absorb both the concept and the mechanics underlying computations. Mental math promotes flexibility in using math facts. Children who are slow in this skill may not really understand the processes taught, or may simply need a great deal more practice.

This center gives children practice in using mental math in the four basic math functions—addition, subtraction, multiplication, and division—testing their mastery of each as they apply to liquid, length, time and counting measurements.

Directions for Making the Center

1. For the background use posterboard, a bulletin board, or room divider. Place the heading, Math Gymnastics, on it.

2. Make seven pockets, for the four puzzles, the Answer Forms, the Puzzle Checker, and for the Objective, Materials, Directions, Evaluation, and On Your Own activities. Label each pocket.

3. Make a ditto for the Answer Form and place copies in the pocket (see opposite page).

4. Using index cards or oaktag, make up 16 problems for each puzzle pocket. If possible, use different colors for each set of puzzles for easy replacement in the correct pocket. (You may just use a different colored pen for writing the problems.)

In the corner of each card write the letter and number of the square in which the answer goes on the Answer Form.

5. Make up a Puzzle Checker card for each pocket. Laminate it and put it in its pocket.

Answer Form

NAME _____ GOAL _____ MINS.

DATE _____ STARTING TIME _____

PUZZLE NO. _____ FINISHING TIME _____

ACTUAL TIME _____ MINS.

M　　　A　　　T　　　H

1	2	3	4
5	6	7	8
9	10	11	12
13	14	15	16

Totals				

6. *Sample directions for Puzzle 1:*

M - 1	1 hr.	= _____ mins.
A - 2	1½ ft.	= _____ in.
T - 3	1 yd. 9 in.	= _____ in.
H - 4	60 sec.	= _____ mins.
M - 5	½ hr.	= _____ mins.
A - 6	1 hr. 25 min.	= _____ mins.
T - 7	2 ft. 1 in.	= _____ in.
H - 8	½ ft.	= _____ in.
M - 9	2 min.	= _____ secs.
A - 10	2 days	= _____ hrs.
T - 11	¾ hr.	= _____ mins.
H - 12	1 day	= _____ hrs.
M - 13	1½ mins.	= _____ secs.
A - 14	1 yd. 2 in.	= _____ in.
T - 15	¼ min.	= _____ secs.
H - 15	1 week	= _____ days

Answer Check Sheet for Puzzle 1 (to be kept by teacher):

M	A	T	H
1 60	2 18	3 45	4 1
5 30	6 85	7 25	8 6
9 120	10 48	11 45	12 24
13 90	14 38	15 15	16 7

300	189	130	38

Puzzle Checker - Puzzle 1

Your answers are correct if:

1. All the numbers in the M column end in 0 *and* their total equals the number of seconds in 5 minutes.

2. All the numbers in the A column contain an 8 *and*

their total equals the number of minutes in 3 hours and 9 minutes.

3. All the numbers in the T column contain a 5 *and* their total equals the sum of A-6 and T-11.

4. The total of all the numbers in the H column is the same as A-14.

7. *Directions for Puzzle 2:*

M - 1	½ pt.	= _____ oz.
A - 2	2½ doz. eggs	= _____
T - 3	2 qts.	= _____ oz.
H - 4	1/3 doz. apples	= _____
M - 5	½ doz. oranges	= _____
A - 6	3 doz. bananas	= _____
T - 7	½ gal.	= _____ qts.
H - 8	1 qt.	= _____ oz.
M - 9	1 gal.	= _____ qts.
A - 10	1½ gal.	= _____ qts.
T - 11	2 pts.	= _____ qts.
H - 12	¾ qt.	= _____ oz.
M - 13	1½ doz. grapes	= _____
A - 14	¾ doz. peaches	= _____
T - 15	16 oz.	= _____ lb.
H - 16	1 pt.	= _____ oz.

Answer Check Sheet for Puzzle 2 (to be kept by teacher):

M	A	T	H
1 8	2 30	3 64	4 4
5 6	6 36	7 2	8 32
9 4	10 6	11 1	12 24
13 18	14 9	15 1	16 16

36	81	68	76

Puzzle Checker - Puzzle 2

Your answers are correct if the total of:
1. Column M is the same as A-6.
2. Column A is the same as A-14 x 9.
3. Column T is the same as the sum of T-3 plus H-4.
4. Column H is the same as A-2 x 2 plus H-16.

8. *Directions for Puzzle 3:*

M - 1	4 x 4 + 7	= _____
A - 2	7 + 2 x 3	= _____
T - 3	7 x 7 + 4	= _____
H - 4	8 x 8 + 3	= _____
M - 5	8 x 6 - 7	= _____
A - 6	12 - 6 x 8	= _____
T - 7	6 x 7 - 5	= _____
H - 8	5 x 7 - 6	= _____
M - 9	10 - 5 x 9	= _____
A - 10	8 ÷ 4 + 5	= _____
T - 11	4 x 7 + 8	= _____
H - 12	4 x 4 + 8	= _____
M - 13	14 ÷ 7 x 9	= _____
A - 14	6 ÷ 2 x 3	= _____
T - 15	10 ÷ 2 - 3	= _____
H - 16	9 ÷ 3 + 9	= _____

Answer Check Sheet for Puzzle 3 (to be kept by teacher):

M	A	T	H
1 23	2 27	3 53	4 67
5 41	6 48	7 37	8 29
9 45	10 7	11 36	12 40
13 18	14 9	15 2	16 12

127	91	128	148

Puzzle Checker - Puzzle 3

Your answers are correct if the total of:
1. Column M is equal to 3 x 9 + 100.
2. Column A is equal to 9 x 9 + 10.
3. Column T is equal to 4 x 7 + 100.
4. Column H is equal to 6 x 8 + 100.

---

9. *Directions for Puzzle 4:*

M - 1	1 kilometer	= _____	meters
A - 2	1½ meters	= _____	centimeters
T - 3	1500 millimeters	= _____	meters
H - 4	2 decameters	= _____	meters
M - 5	2 kilograms	= _____	grams
A - 6	1 meter	= _____	centimeters
T - 7	5000 grams	= _____	kilograms
H - 8	3000 milligrams	= _____	grams
M - 9	10 meters	= _____	centimeters
A - 10	2 liters	= _____	centiliters
T - 11	3 meters	= _____	decimeters
H - 12	2½ kilometers	= _____	meters
M - 13	1 kiloliter	= _____	liters
A - 14	1000 milliliters	= _____	centiliters
T - 15	500 milligrams	= _____	grams
H - 16	2 grams	= _____	milligrams

Answer Check Sheet for Puzzle 4 (to be kept by teacher):

M	A	T	H
1 1000	2 150	3 1½	4 20
5 2000	6 100	7 5	8 3
9 1000	10 200	11 30	12 2500
13 1000	14 10	15 ½	16 2000

5000	460	37	4523

Puzzle Checker - Puzzle 4

Your answers are correct if the total of the:
1. M column equals 1000 x 5.
2. A column equals 400 + 30 + 30.
3. T column equals 15 x 2 + 7.
4. H column equals 4000 + 500 + 20 + 3.

Discussion

This should be an enjoyable center for children who know their math facts. For others it will give needed practice and will suggest skills to review. The center might lead these children to mastery of these facts.

Adjust the content of each of the puzzles to fit the needs of your class. Some of the suggested puzzles may be too easy, some too difficult. You might want to concentrate strongly upon the metric system if children need it.

Make this an on-going center by making up new puzzles, or by getting children to do so, for the puzzle pockets.

This center encourages the children to use self-reliance and perseverance in checking their work. Permit those children who need it to use the Answer Check Sheets.

Classification

LEARNING CENTER NO. 18   SOCIAL STUDIES LEVELS K-1

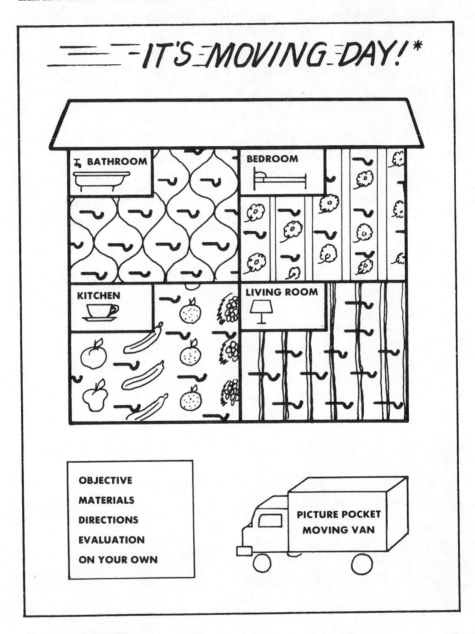

*Developed from ideas contributed by Susan Fierko.

IT'S MOVING DAY!

For the Student

Objective

To put all the things that belong in a house in their right places.

Materials

You will need: scissors, oaktag, paste or glue, a hole punch, old magazines.

Directions

1. Pretend it's moving day. Take a picture from the Moving Van Picture Pocket.

2. Find the room in the house where the thing on the picture belongs. Hang the picture on a hook in the room where it belongs.

3. Hang all the pictures from the moving van in the rooms where they belong.

Evaluation

Check your work. Look at the back of each picture that you hung up. See if the symbol on the back of the picture matches the symbol for the room where you put it.

On Your Own

1. Get some magazines.

2. Cut out pictures for each room in the house.

3. Cut pieces of oaktag. Make them the same size as the cards in the Moving Van Picture Pocket.

4. Paste each picture you cut out on a card.

5. Punch a hole in the top center of each card.

6. Draw the correct symbol on the back of each card to show which room it belongs in.

7. Hang each card in the room where it belongs.

8. Show your work to your teacher (or to a classmate).

9. Take your cards off the hooks and put them in the Moving Van Picture Pocket.

Suggestions for the Teacher—Learning Center No. 18

Objectives

One of the important cognitive skills that children develop at increasingly complex levels of performance is the ability to classify and categorize various kinds of data. This skill involves: sensation—using the senses to know what things look, feel, taste, act like; perception—distinguishing likenesses and differences; and conception—generalizing what constitutes a grouping. The objective is to make children more discriminatingly aware of the world around them, and more thoughtful about the underlying order or structure.

Directions for Making the Center

1. Draw the house on a large sheet of posterboard or cardboard that has been painted or covered with colored contact or construction paper.

2. Use a wallpaper sample book (or any other source of patterns) and cut out squares that might be appropriate for each room. Mount them as the background for each quadrant. In the upper left-hand corner of each quadrant, mount a symbol to indicate which room it is, e.g. ⊓ living room, ⊨══╡ bedroom, ☕ kitchen, ⟐══⟐ bathroom.

3. Using drapery hooks, stick the sharp point of each through the board. Place six to ten hooks in each room.

4. Cut out pictures of household objects commonly found in each of these rooms and paste each picture to a 5" x 6" card made of oaktag. Cover each picture with clear contact paper or laminate it. Punch a hole through the center top of each card.

5. On the back of each picture, place the symbol for each room for self-checking.

6. Using oaktag (or a manila envelope), make a picture

pocket. Glue or staple it to the board. Insert all picture cards. You can make this pocket look like a moving van.

7. Using oaktag (or a manila envelope), make another pocket. Label it: Objective, Materials, Directions, Evaluation, On Your Own, and glue or staple it to the board. Insert the appropriate instruction sheets for the children in this pocket.

Discussion

Before working independently, the children will have had experiences playing in the housekeeping corner; with doll house furniture; with dramatic play; with pictures and stories.

Young children will have to have the teacher (or aide) read the instructions to them.

To promote reading, each card in the picture pocket may be labeled with the name of the object shown.

The teacher may post a list of the names of children who have successfully completed this learning center, and these children may serve to check the work of children new to this task.

The picture cards created by the children should be checked by the teacher and added to the picture pocket. New pictures should be added by the teacher periodically.

This center may be followed up by other centers involving classification skills, such as: zoo animals, farm animals, pets; clothing for summer, winter, rain or snow; land, air and water vehicles, etc.

Directions

LEARNING CENTER NO. 19　　　SOCIAL STUDIES LEVELS 4-6

CENTERVILLE

For the Student

Objective

At this center you will find your way to different locations using the eight major compass headings on a map.

Materials

You will need a pencil and paper.

Directions

1. Start by reading the directions for Scramble 1. Using the Centerville map, follow the directions carefully.

2. Write your answers on a separate sheet of paper. Be sure to write your name, the date and the learning center number at the top.

3. Check your answers with the answer card. You will find it in the pocket on the back cover of this center.

4. Now do Scramble 2.

Evaluation

Use the answer cards to check your work whenever possible.

Put your answer sheet in your folder. Your teacher will go over it with you during your conference.

On Your Own

1. Do two of the tasks in the Task Cards pocket.

2. When you have finished, do as many more as you like. Your teacher will check your work. Maybe he will add the tasks you made up to the center for your classmates to do.

Centerville

Directions for Scramble 1

You are visiting your grandmother, who lives on Avenue E, corner 7th Street, in Centerville. You go out for a walk just to explore the neighborhood.

You walk 1 block east, 2 blocks south, 3 blocks east, 1 block north, ½ block east. You are delighted to find that you are at the _____. You go in and look around.

When you come out, you go directly home. You walk 1 block north and 4 blocks _____.

When you get home, your grandmother asks you to go to the supermarket to buy some groceries for her. She tells you to walk 2 blocks east, then 2½ blocks south. But after you have walked 4½ blocks, you find that you are at a flower shop.

You retrace your steps, and this time you find the right store. What mistake did you make the first time?

CENTERVILLE

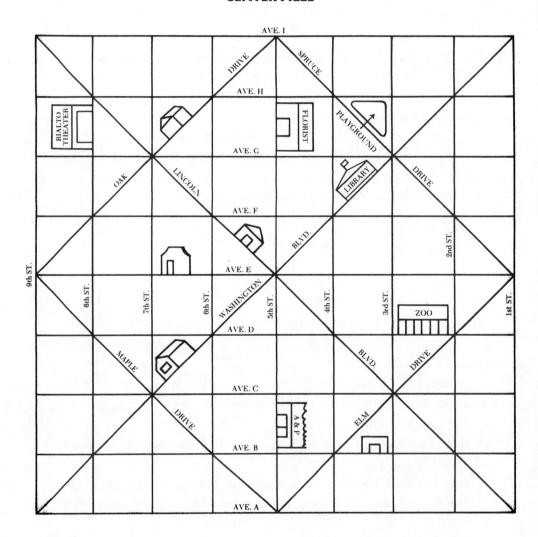

Centerville

Directions for Scramble 2

A friend telephones and invites you over for lunch. She tells you to walk 2 blocks north and ½ block northeast to get to her house. What street does she live on? _____

After lunch you go to the library together. You walk northeast for ½ block. Then you turn east. What street are you on? _____

You walk east for 3 blocks. Then you turn south. What street are you on now? _____

You walk one block and then go southwest. How far is it to the library from your friend's house? _____

When you come out of the library, your friend walks you home. You walk southwest for 1½ blocks. On Avenue E you turn _____ to get home.

Your friend drops you off at your grandmother's house. Then she walks north for 2 blocks and turns _____ for ½ block to get to her house.

If your friend had wanted to take a shorter way home, she could have left you at the corner of Washington Blvd. and 5th Street. You would have continued to your grandmother's house alone, and she could have walked northwest on Lincoln Blvd. to Oak Drive. How many blocks shorter would it have been for her this way? _____ How many blocks would you have had to walk alone? _____

On Your Own Task Cards

TASK CARD 1

Start at Avenue B and 3rd Street. Go 2 blocks west; then turn north. Stop and buy some peanuts. Continue north to Avenue D; then turn east. Go feed the peanuts to a monkey. Where will you go? _____ How far did you walk all together? _____

Now go north on 2nd Street to Avenue F. Go northwest for 1½ blocks. Where are you? _____

Have a ride on a swing. Then continue northwest to 5th Street. Then go southwest to 8th Street. What street did you take? _____ How many blocks did you walk on this street? _____

Go north until you come to the movie house. What street is it on? _____ Between what two streets? _____ Go in and see the show. Enjoy yourself.

TASK CARD 2
Start at Lincoln Blvd. and Avenue G. Go southeast to 5th Street. Then go south to Avenue A. Then go back north on 5th Street to Avenue E. Then go northeast on Washington Blvd. to Avenue G. Stop and rest. Count up how many blocks you walked all together. _____

What letter did the path you walked make? _____

TASK CARD 3
You met a girl at the playground and you invited her to visit you at your grandmother's house. She lives on Avenue B between 3rd Street and 4th Street.

Write two different sets of directions for her to get from her house to your house. Tell which directions are easier. Tell which directions give the shorter route.

TASK CARD 4
Start out any place on the map and trace a square of any size with your finger.

Now write directions so that someone else can follow your square path. Be sure to tell where to begin.

Give your directions to one of your classmates. See if he can follow them correctly.

TASK CARD 5
Start out any place on the map. Trace a triangle of any size with your finger.

Now write directions so that someone else can make the same triangle. Be sure to tell where to begin.

Give your directions to one of your classmates. See if he can follow them correctly.

TASK CARD 6

What are your initials? See if you can trace a path on the map with your finger that will form your first initial. Write directions for this path.

Do the same for your last initial.

Give your directions to one of your classmates. See if he can figure out what letters the paths he followed made.

Scramble 1 Answers

zoo

west

You went north instead of south

Scramble 2 Answers

Oak Drive

Ave H

3rd Street

5 blocks (½ NE, 3 E, 1 S, ½ SW)

west

NE

2 blocks shorter (with you: 1½ SW, 2 W, 2 N, ½ NE; short cut: 1½ SW, 2 NW, ½ NE)

2 blocks

Task Card 1 Answers

to the zoo

6½ blocks

at the playground

Oak Drive

3 blocks

8th Street

Ave. G and Ave. H

Task Card 2 Answers

12 blocks (2 SE, 4 S, 4 N, 2 NE)

Y

Suggestions for the Teacher—Learning Center No. 19

Objectives

Map reading using the eight major directions is an important skill which takes a lot of practice. The students will have been introduced to these skills previously. This center helps to reinforce the skills through game-like activities.

Being able to follow and give precise directions is an important survival skill. This center also aids the student in this area. It provides progressively more difficult tasks in following directions. It also has children try their hand at writing directions of their own.

Directions for Making the Center

1. Create a Centerville map.

2. Write a set of directions using only the four major directions. This will be Scramble 1.

3. Create another set of directions using all eight major directions. This will be Scramble 2.

4. This center is mounted on a posterboard folded in book fashion. On the front cover, place the center number and title. Provide two pockets. One pocket holds the general directions. In the other pocket, place the Centerville map and the directions for Scramble 1.

5. On the inside front cover, place the directions for Scramble 2 in a pocket.

6. Make up a number of task cards. On oaktag or index cards, write directions varying in complexity. Place these On Your Own Task Cards in a pocket on the inside back cover.

7. Some of the activities have fixed answers. Make up answer cards for these and place them in a pocket on the back cover.

8. Laminate (or cover with contact paper) all directions and tasks.

Discussion

Through direct teaching, and through real-life experiences in and out of school, children begin to master the skills of map reading and of following directions. This center is adaptable to any level and is very useful in providing needed practice in comprehension and use of map skills. The Centerville map may be made as simple or as complex as is appropriate for any particular group of children. Only the basic skills are illustrated here, but other features may be included as they are introduced in class. The remaining eight compass headings may be added, as may various keys and legends and mileage markers.

The children will, of course, have had experiences making maps and plans of the school, the school neighborhood, and their home neighborhoods. Working with home-made maps and plans is excellent preparation for interpreting actual road maps, atlases and globes.

The Newspaper

LEARNING CENTER NO. 20   SOCIAL STUDIES LEVELS 5-6

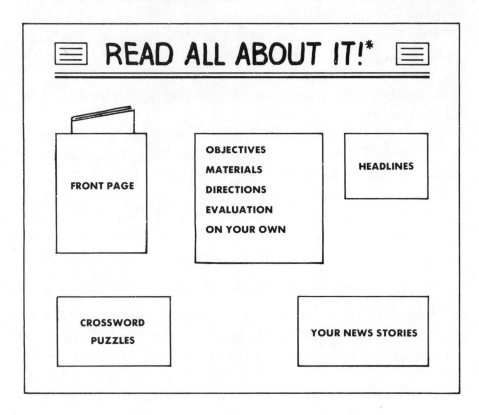

READ ALL ABOUT IT

For the Student

Objectives

You will use newspapers to improve your current events vocabulary.

You will improve your skills of word analysis.

---

*Developed from ideas contributed by Joan Carlson.

Materials

You will need newspaper pages, writing paper, a dictionary.

Directions

1. Select one of the newspaper pages from the pocket.

2. On a sheet of paper list all the headlines. Next to each headline, indicate whether it deals with international, national or local news.

3. Scan some of the items on the page and select ten words that are unfamiliar to you. List them on another sheet of paper. Examine each word. Draw a line under the root of the word, and a circle around any prefixes or suffixes.

Reread the sentence in which the word was used. Try to guess at the meaning. Write your own definition next to each word.

Now check each word in the dictionary. Correct any of your definitions if you need to. (Watch out for words that have more than one meaning. Find the meaning that fits in your particular newspaper story.)

4. Select a puzzle from the Crossword Puzzles pocket and try to solve it.

5. Using five of your ten new words, make your own crossword puzzle. When you have finished, make a copy and put it in the Crossword Puzzles pocket. Be sure to put your name on your puzzle. Keep your answer key.

Evaluation

1. Look for a number in the upper right-hand corner of the newspaper page you chose. In the Headline pocket there is an answer sheet with this number on it. Check your headline classifications.

2. Use the dictionary to check your word meanings, roots, prefixes and suffixes. If you need help, consult your teacher.

3. Find the person whose name was on the crossword puzzle you chose. Ask him for the answer key and check your work.

On Your Own

1. Write a newspaper headline using each one of your ten new words. Your headline can deal with news about something outside school; or it can deal with some school news; or it can deal with some class news.

2. Select three articles from the Your News Stories pocket. On a sheet of paper, write the headline of each story. Then give your reactions to the story—comment on both the content and the style of the writing.

3. Choose one of the ten headlines you wrote using your new words. Write a newspaper article about it. When you have finished, correct your own work for spelling and grammar and then put your article in the Your News Stories pocket.

Suggestions for the Teacher—Learnining Center No. 20

Objectives

In a democratic society, developing the habit of reading a daily newspaper is vital. To encourage students to do this, their interest has to be aroused, and their confidence in their ability has to be gradually built up. This activity works on some of the component skills, and relates a school newspaper to the real adult newspaper.

Vocabulary growth is promoted by encouraging the use of context clues and structural analysis to guess at word meanings before using a dictionary for precise definition and for selecting an appropriate meaning.

Directions for Making the Center

1. Make this a permanent center by mounting it where it can be kept for a long period of time. A bulletin board or room divider would be appropriate. Colorful pictures and clippings of interesting news events mounted on the center will make it more attractive. Change these frequently to keep them current.

2. Select the pages from the newspaper judiciously, keeping in mind content, and level of complexity. Avoid pages with a

great number of items. Number each newspaper page in the upper right-hand corner and provide an answer key for headline classifications. Change the pages (and answers) frequently.

3. The children will have had previous experiences solving crossword puzzles and making up puzzles of their own. Still, it is a good idea to display a sample at the center, such as:

DOWN
1. One complete turn or rotation.

ACROSS
2. Something that comes out of a volcano.
3. Head of a Moslem state.
4. Bravery, determination.
5. A special kind of can, as for insect spray.

Answers have been inserted into the puzzle here just for illustration. For classroom use, put the answers in a Word Bank.

Discussion

This particular center lends itself to children's working in pairs. The teacher may choose to add this option in the directions to the student (i.e., If you would like, find a partner who would like to work with you at this activity center).

Another possibility is that the teacher, having observed during vocabulary work which children are particularly alert to word analysis, posts a list of Vocabulary Helpers. Then children can show their completed work to one of the students on this list to be checked out. (Similar lists may be made for other specific skills, thus developing a peer helping atmosphere.)

Publishing a class newspaper is a rewarding activity. Children can take turns serving as reporters, typists, ditto operators, editors, proofreaders. Some of the items in Your News Stories should be selected for publication.

Leaves

LEARNING CENTER NO. 21   SCIENCE LEVELS K-1

LEAVES FOR EVERYONE

For the Student

Objective

You will make a leaf collection.

Materials

You will need leaves, paper, paste, crayons, an iron, wax paper, leaf reference books, wire hanger, string.

Directions

1. Bring in leaves from your neighborhood. Try to get at least six different kinds of leaves.

2. Lay all your leaves on the table. Put all the leaves that are the same color together.

How many different groups do you have? _____

What colors do you have? _____ What color do you like best? _____

Show your leaves to a classmate. Ask him which color he likes best. _____

3. Arrange your leaves in a row by size, with the smallest leaf first and the largest leaf last. Ask a classmate to look at your row of leaves. Does he agree with you about their size? _____

4. Look at each leaf. What shape does it look like? Take the leaf shape cards from the pocket. Lay a shape card beside each leaf. Get a friend to look at your cards. Does he agree with you? _____

5. Get some paper. Trace around each of your leaves on a separate sheet of paper.

Get one of the reference books. See if you can find each leaf and its name. Look in the Leaf Words pocket. Find the card for your leaf. Copy the name of your leaf below your tracing.

Write your name on each paper. Put all your papers in the basket. Your teacher will check to see if you have named all your leaves correctly.

6. Get a sheet of wax paper. Place one of your leaves on it.

Get a small piece of white paper. Write the name of the leaf and your own name on it. Place it below the leaf.

Sprinkle some chips of crayon on the wax paper and leaf.

Get another piece of wax paper. Place it on top of the leaf and the name slip. Get the iron and press until the two pieces of wax paper have stuck together.

Do the same thing for each of your leaves.

Tack your wax tracings up on the bulletin board at this center.

Evaluation

Your classmates or your teacher will check the color, size, and shape arrangements of your leaves.

Check the names of your leaves by looking at the papers hanging on the bulletin board.

On Your Own

1. Make a beautiful leaf book. Cut pictures of leaves and trees out of magazines. Put real leaves in your book or draw or trace leaves. Try to identify as many leaves and trees by name as you can.

2. Make a leaf mobile. Use the string and a wire hanger. Hang it in the classroom or in your own home.

3. Find one special tree near your home or near school that you like very much. Draw it the way it looks now. Write the date on your drawing. Keep your drawing in your folder. A few months from now, look at your tree. Has it changed? If it has, make a new drawing and date it. Every few months check your tree to see if it has changed.

Suggestions for the Teacher—Learning Center No. 21

Objectives

This center encourages children to observe their everyday environment, noting differences in colors, shapes, and sizes. It gives practice in perceptual and motor skills.

This center also encourages children to use reference books on a very simple level to identify leaves they have collected.

Children also engage in a creative experience as they mount their creations for display.

Directions for Making the Center

1. This is a very easy center to construct, for in essence, the

children make most of it as they hang their work up for display.

Choose a bulletin board, divider, or other large flat surface for the background. Use cut-out letters to make the heading, Leaves for Everyone.

2. Print or type the Objectives, Materials, Evaluation, and On Your Own on oaktag. Make enough copies of the Directions so each child can have his own. Insert into a pocket or envelope mounted at a low level for children to reach.

3. Using oaktag, cut shapes such as: *oval, circle, square, rectangle, diamond.* Insert these into a Shapes pocket or envelope.

4. On oaktag, strips, write the names of the common leaves found in your neighborhood, such as: maple, oak, elm, dogwood, sycamore, walnut, etc. Insert in the Leaf Words pocket or envelope.

5. For visual appeal, collect a number of colorful leaves of various shapes and sizes and paste them on the bulletin board.

6. Cut up some shavings from old crayons, placing them in a container for use in making the wax mountings.

7. As children complete their products they mount them on the bulletin board. They may also hang on or near it their leaf mobiles.

8. Provide the materials the children will need—pencils, paper, wax paper, crayons, iron, paste, string, hangers.

9. Include books or encyclopedias that have pictures of leaves along with their names. Particularly recommended are: Anne Ophelia Dowden, *Wild Green Things in the City, A Book of Weeds*, New York, Crowell, 1972; Edward Gallob, *City Leaves, City Trees*, New York, Scribner, 1972; Millicent Selsam and Joyce Hunt, *A First Look at Leaves*, New York, Walker, 1972; and F.K. Makins, *Identification of Trees and Shrubs*, New York, Dutton, 1949.

Discussion

This center is designed for very young children and considerable guidance and explanation may be required. It may be necessary to read the directions to the children several times.

This is a challenging center for young children. It requires the completion of more than one task and involves working independently for an extended period of time. However, the activities are manipulative and of high interest and should engage the child for a somewhat long stretch.

It would be a good idea to use this center as a follow-up to a field experience where trees and leaves are looked at and discussed. The fall would be a desirable time to introduce this center.

Commercially prepared or home-made slides or filmstrips of trees and leaves would enhance this center.

It will be important to demonstrate the process of making wax rubbings of the leaves, with special emphasis on the safety features to practice when using the iron. Be sure the iron is always set on a low heat, and unplugged when not in use.

A branch from a tree might be brought into the classroom. Children could hang some of their leaves on this branch, creating an original tree.

In addition to comments and suggestions to individuals as they do their work, hold a class discussion when everyone has finished. Give everyone a chance to show off his work. Show some leaves for children to identify. Discuss the seasons of the year and how leaves change. Compile a list of all the leaves found in the neighborhood. Make graphs showing the number of leaves collected of various varieties.

Classification

LEARNING CENTER NO. 22   SCIENCE LEVELS 2-3

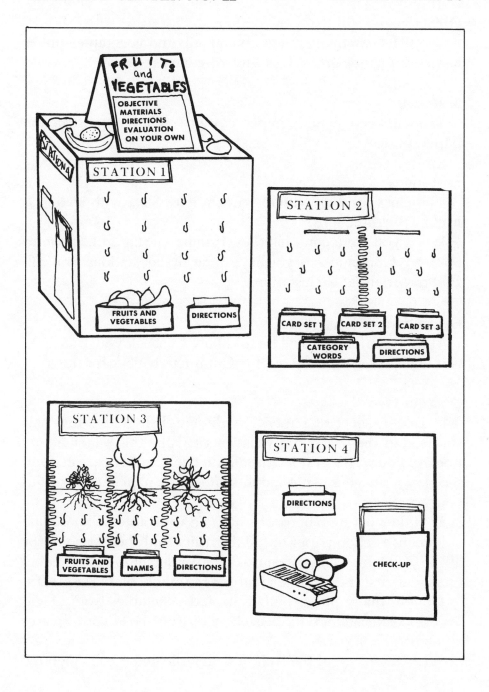

FRUITS AND VEGETABLES

For the Student

Objective

You will learn many things about fruits and vegetables—their names, how they grow, how and why we eat them.

Materials

You will need: pencils, paper, cassette recorder, construction paper, paste.

Directions

This center is divided into four stations. Start with Station 1. Follow the directions.

When you have completed everything at Station 1, go on to Station 2. Continue until you have done all four stations. You will find directions at each station.

Evaluation

At each station you will be told how to check your work. As you do each activity, fill out the Completed Work form.

On Your Own

1. Take a sheet of paper. Divide it in half. Label one half FRUITS, and the other half VEGETABLES. Take this paper home. Look in your refrigerator. List all the fruits and vegetables you see in it. Write your name and the date on the paper and give it to your teacher.

2. Make your own book of fruits and vegetables. Choose one color construction paper for all the fruits, and another color for all the vegetables. Cut the construction paper into squares. Label one square FRUITS, and one square of the other color VEGETABLES.

Cut out many pictures of fruits and vegetables from magazines or seed catalogs. Paste each picture on one of your squares of construction paper.

Write the name of the fruit or vegetable under each picture.

Punch holes in each piece of construction paper. Tie a piece of wool in the holes. Hang your book on the bulletin board.

3. Make a book about your favorite fruit and vegetable. Answer the questions on this form. Use the books at this center to find the information.

	My favorite fruit is	My favorite vegetable is
Where does it grow best?		
When should it be planted?		
How long does it take to grow?		
How much light, sun, water does it need?		
What can spoil its growth?		

If it is possible, plant seeds for your favorite fruit and vegetable. Keep a fruit and vegetable diary for your plants telling when you watered them, what growth you observed. Find recipes for different ways of eating them.

Put your book in your folder. Show it to your teacher during your conference.

4. In each of the sentences below there is hidden the name of the fruit. When you find it, draw a circle around it.

Put your completed paper in your folder.

Example: Please remember, rye bread for Tom and white bread for Mary.

  a. All the children who knew the answer were raising their hands.

  b. "Clap, please," the announcer said to the TV audience.

  c. "Please wait for me. It won't take me long to get ready."

  d. She is a little deaf, so when you knock on her door, give a big rap, especially if you hear that her TV is on.

  e. We hope a check will be made to see that everything is safe.

f. My teacher always smiles and never shows disappointment or anger.

g. He lost his belt, so he tied a rope around his waist.

h. She wore a turban, an ankle bracelet and a peasant skirt for the costume party.

Hidden Fruit Answers

a. raisin   e. peach

b. apple   f. orange

c. melon   g. pear

d. grapes   h. banana

Suggestions for the Teacher—Learning Center No. 22

Objectives

This center takes children through some simple stages of identifying, naming, classifying, evaluating fruits and vegetables. The activities are designed to enable children to make observations and form concepts such as: all fruits and vegetables are plants used for food; although they differ in many ways (size, shape, color, where they grow, how they may be eaten) they have certain things in common; fruits have their seeds visibly within them; it is important for our health to eat fruits and vegetables.

Directions for Making the Center

1. You can add variety to the appearance of the centers in your classroom by using a cardboard box for this center. Obtain a reasonably good sized box and paint it colorfully or cover it with colorful contact or construction paper. Each of the four sides is used for one of the stations.

2. To make the heading for the top of the box, use a piece of posterboard or cardboard folded into an inverted V-shape. Print

Fruits and Vegetables
Completed Work

Name   *Date*

STATION 1

1. _____ checked my work. I got _____ right.
2. We played _____. _____ won.

STATION 2

1. CARD SET 1:   I got _____ right.
2. CARD SET 2:   I got _____ right.
3. CARD SET 3:   I got _____ right.

STATION 3

1. _____ checked my work. I got _____ right.
2. We played Concentration. _____ won.

STATION 4

I _____ the story about Rickety Ricky.
(liked, didn't like)

ON YOUR OWN

I did numbers _____.

FRUITS and VEGETABLES (or use letter cut-outs) on both sides of the V. Make a pocket for the Objectives, Materials, Directions, Evaluation, On Your Own. (Additional directions and evaluation techniques are included at each station.) Tape the V to the top of the box.

3. Run off copies of the Completed Work form and put them in the directions pocket.

4. *Station 1*   Draw or cut out pictures of fruits and vegetables such as: apple, banana, cantaloupe, grapefruit, grapes, orange, peach, pear, carrot, celery, corn, lettuce, onion, peas, potato, radish. (At this stage, avoid items like tomatoes, cucumbers, strawberries.) Paste each picture on a card. Punch a hole in the top middle of each card. Insert 16 drapery hooks into this side of the box. Hang the pictures on the drapery hooks.

On separate cards, draw a picture of each of these fruits and vegetables in cross-section. Make one more card labeled Fruits and Vegetables. Attach an envelope or pocket to the bottom of this side of the box. Put this set of cards in this pocket.

Make another pocket for the directions to the pupil.

Directions for Station 1

1. Take the set of Fruits and Vegetables cards from the pocket. Match each of these pictures with a picture on the hooks. Hang them up.

2. Get a friend to check your work.

3. Take all the pictures off the hooks. Mix them up. Play Old Maid or Go Fish with your friend using the pairs of cards.

4. Put the pictures of the whole fruits and vegetables back on the hooks. Put the other pictures back in the pocket.

5. Go on to Station 2.

---

5. *Station 2*   Attach three envelopes to the bottom of Station 2. Label them: Card Set 1, Card Set 2, Card Set 3. Cutting pictures out of magazines and catalogs, make up three different sets of cards with 16 cards in each set. Set 1 should consist of pictures of toys and foods, such as: accordian, baseball, blocks, doll, dollhouse, football, jack-in-the-box, soldiers, bread, cake,

cereal, eggs, frankfurter, milk, pineapple, tomato. On the back of each card, put a small T or F depending on whether it is a toy or a food.

Set 2 should consist of eight different balls, such as: a baseball, basketball, beach ball, bowling ball, football, ping pong ball, tennis ball, volley ball, and eight different kinds of dolls. On the back of each card, put a small B or D.

Set 3 should duplicate the Fruits and Vegetables cards in Station 1 that show these foods in cross-section. On the back of each card, put a small F or V.

Attach a fourth pocket to the bottom of the box and label it Category Words. Write the words Toys, Foods, Balls, Dolls, Fruits, Vegetables, on strips of construction paper, and put the strips in the pocket.

At the top of the box, make two slits into which the category cards may be inserted. Hang eight drapery hooks on one side of the box and eight hooks on the other side, drawing a partition line between.

Make another pocket for the directions to the pupil.

Directions for Station 2

You know that you have different names by which you may be called or identified. For example, you have your proper name, and you may also have a nickname. You may also be called a boy or a girl, a child, a student, a son or a daughter, a grandchild, or a niece or a nephew.

Other things may also be identified by different names. For example, you may call your pet Brandy; other people may call him an animal, or a dog, or a poodle.

At this center you will classify things in different ways by different names.

Take all the cards out of the pocket labeled Card Set

1. Look at them carefully. Now arrange them in two groups. Hang one group on the hooks on the left-hand side of the station. Hang the other group on the hooks on the right-hand side of the station. Now look in the pocket labeled Category Words. See if you can find words to describe your two groups. Insert these words into the slots above the hooks you hung your pictures on.

Now turn over each of your cards. Look at the letter on the back. Does it match the first letter of the category word you put it under? Check all your cards, changing any you may have gotten wrong. Then put the cards back in the pocket.

Now do the same thing with Card Set 2 and Card Set 3.

When you have finished, put all the cards back in their pocket and go on to Station 3.

---

6. *Station 3*   At the top of the box draw somewhat abstracted symbols for a bush or vine, a tree, and an underground plant. Under the first two symbols insert six hooks; under the last symbol insert four hooks.

Make three pockets at the bottom. Label the first one Fruits and Vegetables, and in it put a duplicate set of cards of the whole fruits and vegetables, as in Station 1.

Write the name of each of the 16 fruits and vegetables depicted on cards. Put them in the second pocket.

In the third pocket put the directions for the pupil.

Directions for Station 3

You know that fruits and vegetables grow on plants of different kinds. At this center you will identify what kind of plant various fruits and vegetables grow on.

Take the cards out of the Fruits and Vegetables pocket. Look at each one. Decide whether you think it grows on a bush or vine, or on a tree, or under the ground. Hang each picture where you think it goes.

Now take all the cards out of the Names pocket. Hang each one on the same hook with the picture it belongs to.

Get someone in your class who has finished this station (or the teacher aide) to check your work.

Take all the cards off the hooks and mix them up. Place them face down in rows on the table. Play Concentration with your classmate (or with the aide). Take turns turning over any two cards. If they are a pair (word and picture match), keep them. If not, turn them back over. See who wins more sets of pairs.

Put all the cards back in the pockets and go on to Station 4.

---

7. *Station 4*   Make up a story to illustrate why we should eat fruits and vegetables, and the different ways that we might eat them. A sample is given. Tape the story and have the cassette and recorder available at this station.

Run off copies of the form for the fruit and vegetable check-up. Put them in a pocket on the station.

Write directions for the pupil and put them in a pocket.

RICKETY RICKY

From the time he was a baby Ricky was a very fussy eater. He only liked certain foods and refused to eat what he did not like. His mother couldn't do a thing with him. She tried to beg him to eat the things he should. He refused. She tried to order him to eat healthy foods. He refused. She tried to bribe him. It didn't work. She tried to fool him by disguising the foods. It didn't work. She tried to punish him. It didn't work.

So she gave up. She let him eat whatever he wanted to. He only wanted to eat ice-cream, cookies, candy, potato chips, soda, hot dogs, ketchup. He wouldn't eat carrots or peas or lettuce or apples or pears or grapefruit. Every day, day after day, he ate only hot dogs and ketchup, and cookies, candy and soda.

Ricky was beginning to grow fatter and fatter. Every time his mother had to buy him new clothes they were a bigger size. He was getting round as a butter ball. Some of the children were beginning to call him Fatso. He didn't feel so good about that.

Also, although he was growing bigger and fatter, he was feeling weaker and weaker. He couldn't run very fast. He always felt tired. He was not very strong.

One morning Ricky woke up feeling very funny. He could hardly get out of bed. He couldn't go to school. His mother was very worried. She took him to the doctor.

The doctor examined Ricky. Then he asked him a lot of questions. He found out all about Ricky's eating habits.

Then the doctor told Ricky and his mother what was wrong. Ricky had what the doctor called "vitamin and mineral deficiencies" because he was not eating the right foods. His muscles and bones were not growing very strong because they were not getting what they needed.

"What can we do?" cried Ricky's mother.

"Well," said the doctor, "I'll have to give Ricky lots of pills to make up for all the things he is not getting in his food. And if that doesn't help, he will have to go into the hospital."

Ricky was worried. He was scared. He was miserable. He did not want to go to the hospital. But he hated to take pills. He hated to take pills more than he hated fruits and vegetables.

"Will I be OK," he asked the doctor, "if I eat lots of fruits and vegetables?"

"Yes, I think so," said the doctor. "It's certainly worth a try."

Ricky and his mother went right to the vegetable market. His mother bought carrots and peas and lettuce and onions and radishes and grapes and apples and pears and grapefruit. When they got home, Ricky's mother prepared many different dishes. She made fruit salad and baked apples and apple sauce and candied carrots and raw carrot strips and fried onions and lettuce with all kinds of dressings.

Ricky looked at all the dishes and made an awful face. But this time he did not refuse to eat them. He was worried about what the doctor had told him. So he began to taste a little.

To his great surprise, nothing was as terrible as he had thought it would be. He even liked some things. Every day he tried a little bit. Pretty soon he discovered what his favorites were and he was happy to eat lots of these. He never refused to try something any more, but always at least tasted it.

Ricky grew thinner even though he was eating more foods. But he grew stronger. Nobody teased him any more. Soon he was able to play all the games the other children were playing. He made lots of friends and was much happier.

When he went back to the doctor for a checkup, the doctor was surprised at how well he looked. He examined him and said, "Nothing wrong with you. I don't want to see you back here for a long, long time."

Directions for Station 4

Get on the tape recorder and listen to the Rickety Ricky story on the cassette.

Did you like the story?

Do you know anyone who is like Ricky?

Are you something like Ricky?

Take a paper from the Checkup pocket. Fill out the form and put it in your folder. Your teacher will go over it with you during your conference.

Now do the On Your Own Activities. They are in the pocket on the top of the box.

Fruit and Vegetable Checkup

Name			Date

FOOD	1 HOW OFTEN	2 IN WHAT FORM	3 LIKES & DISLIKES
Apple			
Banana			
Cantaloupe			
Grapefruit			
Grapes			
Orange			
Peach			
Pear			
Carrot			
Celery			
Corn			
Lettuce			
Onion			
Peas			
Potato			
Radish			

Directions:

COLUMN 1: How often do you eat these foods? Put one of these letters in each box in column 1:

O=more than 3 x a week   R=about once a
                                        month

S=about once a week   N=never

COLUMN 2: Tell how you usually eat each of these
foods. Put one or more of these letters in each box in
column 2:

R=raw   F=fresh   Fr=frozen

C=cooked   Ca=canned

COLUMN 3: Tell whether you like or dislike each of
these foods. Put one of these letters in each box in
column 3:

A=I love it   I=I can take it or leave it

L=I like it   D=I dislike it

H=I hate it

Discussion

Young children are not overly fond of fruits and vegetables.
To motivate them, the activities should be appealing. This
center should not be undertaken until the children have had a
great deal of direct experiences. Visiting a farm, visiting a
supermarket, cooking in school, planting in school, running a
play grocery, all these and more are important prerequisite
activities. The concepts included here tend to be somewhat
oversimplified and the teacher should be cautious about not
misrepresenting. It will take a long time and much more study
and experience for students to develop a scientific interest in
botany. What is important here is that the activities be appropriate for the level, and that the concepts be concretized through
direct experiences so they do not become mechanical verbal
data.

The teacher should see that there is a supply of reference

books available at this center, including a simple encyclopedia (e.g. The Golden Book Encyclopedia), beginner's cookbooks, and simple science books on plants and planting. The seed companies are usually generous about sending catalogs to schools. Some of the companies you might want to write to are: W. Atlee Burpee, Northrup King Seeds, Asgrow Mandeville Co., Inc., Crosman Seed Corporation.

Other class projects should be undertaken to support this center. For example, making a cornucopia with papier-mache fruits and vegetables made by the children, painting seasonal murals, are activities that engage children.

Future stations may explore further the general topic of plants, learning what they need to grow, their parts, etc.

Nutrition

LEARNING CENTER NO. 23   SCIENCE LEVELS 4-6

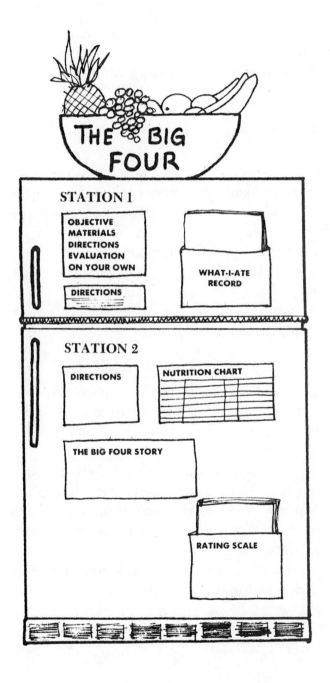

THE BIG FOUR

For the Student

Objective

You will learn about four food groups that nutritionists consider basic to health.

You will decide whether you are eating the proper foods.

Materials

You will need: pencil, paper, old magazines and newspapers.

Directions

1. There are two stations in this center. Start with Station 1 and follow the directions there. When you have finished it, go on to Station 2.

2. Complete the On Your Own activities.

Evaluation

You will compare your answers with your partner. Your teacher will also check your work.

On Your Own

1. Look through old magazines and newspapers. Find pictures of various foods. Organize them according to the Basic Four Food Groups. Make a collage of each food group and display it in the room.

2. Would you change your eating habits if you knew they were not healthy? Name some foods that you probably eat too much of. Name some foods that you do not eat enough of. Write a resolution about some way in which you are willing to change your food habits.

3. Make up a menu of foods you would like for breakfast, lunch, and dinner tomorrow that would meet the Basic Four requirements.

4. Write an imaginary story entitled "He Didn't Know about the Basic Four."

Suggestions for the Teacher—Learning Center No. 23

Objectives

In today's world of fast-food restaurant operations and TV dinners, proper food habits are frequently overlooked. Expediency seems to be the rule.

This center acquaints children with some basic concepts in nutrition and encourages them to think about the kinds of things they eat.

The center prepares children for a more in-depth treatment of nutrition. Subsequent centers may be planned to explore food properties—carbohydrates, proteins, fats, minerals, vitamins, and calories—which are barely touched upon here.

Directions for Making the Center

1. For the background obtain a large piece of cardboard. Decorate it as a refrigerator as in the sketch. Place pictures or drawings of foods at strategic spots.

2. Use cereal or cracker boxes to make the various pockets at this center.

3. Have a supply of magazines and newspapers on hand for the On Your Own activity.

4. Have books and charts on nutrition available. The U. S. Public Health Service has a wealth of materials you can send for.

5. *Station 1*   Use the upper part of your refrigerator. Print or type the directions on a card. Paste it to the center. Make a ditto of the What I Ate Record and insert copies into a cereal box pocket mounted on the center.

Directions for Station 1

At this center you are going to examine the kinds of foods you eat and judge whether you are eating too much or too little of some foods. Before you do anything else at this center, take one of the What-I-Ate

---

Record Sheets from the pocket and for one whole day keep a list of everything you eat and drink. Try to record exactly how much you ate, such as: one large apple, 8 oz. of milk, one 3 oz. hamburger, one cinnamon bun, etc. When you have finished your list, bring it back to this center and go on to Station 2.

What-I-Ate Record

NAME _____   DATE _____

BREAKFAST *Time* ____	LUNCH *Time* _____
Food *Amount*	*Food* *Amount*
DINNER *Time* _____	BETWEEN MEAL SNACKS
Food *Amount*	*Food* *Time* *Amount*

---

6. *Station 2*   Use the lower part of your refrigerator. Print or type the directions, the Big Four Story, and the Nutrition Chart on colored paper and paste them to the background. Use a cereal box for the Rating Scale.

Directions for Station 2

Pair up with a friend and do these activities:
1. Read the Big Four Story. Try to memorize the Basic Four food groups. Think of your own eating habits as you read.
2. Now study the Nutrition Chart. Notice the different foods in each of the Basic Four groups. See if you

can find out what constitutes one serving for the different foods.

3. Each of you get a Rating Scale from the pocket. You will need it as you do the rest of the activities for this station. When you complete the form, put it in your folder. Your teacher will go over it with you later.

RATING SCALE

_____   _____
                    Name   *Date*

ACTIVITY 1   My eating habits are

_____
Bad   Fair   Good

Tell why:

ACTIVITY 2   Joe's eating habits are

_____
Bad   Fair   Good

Tell why:

ACTIVITY 3   Steve's eating habits are

_____
Bad   Fair   Good

Tell why:

ACTIVITY 4   Susan's eating habits are

Bad   Fair   Good

Tell why:

Activity 1

Examine the What I Ate Record you made for Station 1. Analyze it, using what you have learned about the Basic Four. With your partner, discuss these questions:

What foods did you eat too much of?

What foods did you not eat enough of?

How do you need to change your eating habits?

When you have finished your discussion, fill in your rating scale for Activity 1 by placing an X at the point on the line which best describes your eating habits. Then, write a paragraph explaining what was right and what was wrong with the foods you ate. Tell whether you fulfilled the requirements for the Four Food Groups.

Activity 2

Yesterday, Joe, a fourth grader, ate these foods: an orange, a bowl of oatmeal, a slice of buttered toast, a steak, a hamburger, a soft drink, a baked potato, and some green peas. Did Joe eat well? Discuss this with your partner. Then fill in the rating scale for Activity 2. Write a paragraph giving your reasons—tell what Joe did both right and wrong.

Activity 3

Steve Silver, a gas station attendant, was very busy yesterday and didn't take time to eat much. For breakfast he had a bowl of cereal and a cup of coffee; for lunch, a steak sandwich and a soft drink; and for dinner, a pizza, a soft drink, and a candy bar. Did

Steve eat well? Discuss this with your partner. Then fill in the rating scale for Activity 3. Write a paragraph telling what was right about Steve's eating and what was wrong.

Activity 4

For breakfast, Susan, who goes to high school, usually drinks a glass of orange juice; for lunch, a sandwich; and for dinner, a bowl of soup and some candy bars. What do you think of Susan's eating habits? Fill in the rating scale for Activity 4 and write a paragraph telling what was wrong with the way she eats. Tell her what she should do to improve.

Activity 5

Suppose your mother asked you about your favorite foods. What are they? Get a sheet of paper and make a list of them. Then, next to each item indicate which of the four basic food groups it belongs in. Do you have some foods in all four groups? If you have no foods in one or more of the groups, write down some foods you think you could learn to enjoy in any of these groups. Show your paper to your mother.

THE BIG FOUR STORY

When you are young, you don't think about your health; you take it for granted. But if you want to live to a healthy, ripe old age, there are certain things you should know and do now. Nutritionists divide the foods we need into groups, known as the Basic Four. If you know about the Basic Four, you might decide to eat foods that will make you as healthy a person as possible.

The Basic Four groups are:

1. The milk group

2. The meat group

3. The vegetable-fruit group

4. The bread-cereal group

People who eat properly will eat something from each of these four food groups every day. If you leave out very much of one or two of the groups, you will not be as healthy as you can be.

To be healthy you have to eat foods that contain the proper amounts of proteins, carbohydrates, fats, minerals, and vitamins. If you eat enough of each of the Basic Four every day, your body will get enough of these important properties.

Have you ever heard people talk about a "balanced diet"? Well, now you might understand that expression better. A person who eats a balanced diet is one who properly selects his foods from all the groups of the Basic Four.

How about sugar? Is it one of the Basic Four? No! But that doesn't mean you should avoid all sweets. Sugar gives calories and is a good source of energy—provided you don't overdo it. Besides, sugar sometimes makes things taste better, like syrup on pancakes, or granulated sugar on cereal. Sugar is necessary but avoid too much of it.

Many of us like to drink soft drinks. They may taste good but they contain too much sugar and not enough minerals, carbohydrates, vitamins, and proteins. A person who understands the Basic Four will not drink too many soft drinks.

Are you a good eater? Do you get your daily share of the Basic Four?

NUTRITION CHART		
The Basic Four	*Examples*	*Amount needed per day for a child*
1. The milk group	Milk, cheese, yogurt, ice cream, cottage cheese, butter, margarine	3 to 5 servings
2. The meat group	Steak, hamburger, pork, liver, chicken, turkey, eggs, peanut butter, dried beans, dried peas, nuts, seafoods	2 or more servings
3. The vegetable-fruit group	All fruits and fruit juices, vebetables	4 or more servings
4. The bread-cereal group	Breakfast cereals, macaroni, noodles, spaghetti, rice, breads, biscuits, grits	4 or more servings

Discussion

Send home a copy of the Nutrition Chart at Station 2 along with an explanation of what you are trying to accomplish with this center. Invite parents to make use of it, to discuss it with their children, to ask you questions about it, and to offer you suggestions as to what you can do at school.

Hold conferences with individual children who seem either

not to grasp the concepts or to be resistant to examining or changing their food habits.

Children might enjoy sharing notes about their food habits. You might encourage discussion and critique of the What I Ate Records.

You might plan another nutrition center on calories in which students learn to count and keep records of calories.

If you have students with a weight problem you might prepare a special center for them on dieting.

Many students are interested in the health foods craze. Another center might be planned around this.

Have a supply of restaurant menus, cookbooks, diet books, and nutrition books around. The *World Book Encyclopedia* has a good article on foods.

Other recommended books are: *.The Pooh Cookbook* by Virginia Ellison (Dutton, 1969); *Fat Free: Common Sense for Young Weight Watchers* (Macmillan, 1975); *Let's Bake Bread* by Hannah L. Johnson (Lathrop, 1973); *Kids are Natural Cooks* prepared by the Parents Nursery School (Houghton Mifflin, 1974); *The First Book of Foods* by Ida Scheib (Watts, 1956); and *The Kids in the Kitchen Cookbook* by Lois Levine (Macmillan, 1968).

A good culmination for this center would be a class luncheon or picnic with children doing the planning to demonstrate their knowledge of the Basic Four.

Eyes

LEARNING CENTER NO. 24   SCIENCE LEVELS 5-6

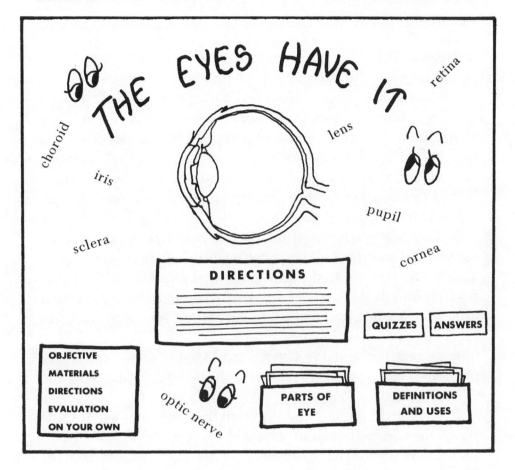

THE EYES HAVE IT

For the Student

Objective

You will do your own research to learn many things about the eye. You will learn the names of the parts of the eye, how the eyes work, and how to take care of your eyes.

Materials

You will need: paper, pencils, encyclopedia, science books, drawing paper, magic markers, flair pens, water colors or crayons, clay, papier-mache, wire, string.

Directions

Pair up with a partner and do these activities together:

1. Take three sheets of paper. Write one of the following headings on each sheet: The Parts of the Eye, How the Eyes Work, How to Take Care of Our Eyes. Use the encyclopedia and any of the science books in your room to find as much information as you can for these three topics. Look in the school library for more books about the eyes if you need more information.

2. Take the cards out of the Parts of the Eye pocket. Check the list you made to see if you have included all these words. Add any words you omitted. Now take the cards out of the other pocket. Match the parts of the eye with their definitions and uses. Check your answers by looking at the backs of the cards to see if each pair has the same numeral.

3. Take a copy of the Crossword Puzzle from the Quizzes pocket. When you have finished, check your work with the answer card.

4. Get the diagram of the eye from the Quizzes pocket. Write down the name of each of the eight parts of the eye next to its number. When you have finished, get the Answer Card from the Answers pocket. Check your work.

5. Make a model eye. You can find instructions in the *World Book Encyclopedia* or in one of the science books in your classroom or in the school library. When you have completed your model, place it on the display table. Each student pair will be given a chance to explain and demonstrate their model to the class.

6. Study the reference sources and compile a list of suggestions for taking care of the eyes. Make an attractive chart about

ACROSS
1. Middle coat of eye
4. Colored part of eye
5. Tear producing glands
7. Opening in eye through which light enters
9. Transparent outer coat of eyeball
10. Part of the eye that forms the picture

DOWN
2. Nerve from eye to brain
3. Eye muscle
5. Fold of skin over eye
6. Part of the eye that receives images
8. White outer membrane of eye

Crossword Puzzle Answers

ACROSS
1. Choroid
4. Iris
5. Lachrymal
7. Pupil
9. Cornea
10. Lens

DOWN
2. Optic
3. Ciliary
5. Lid
6. Retina
8. Sclera

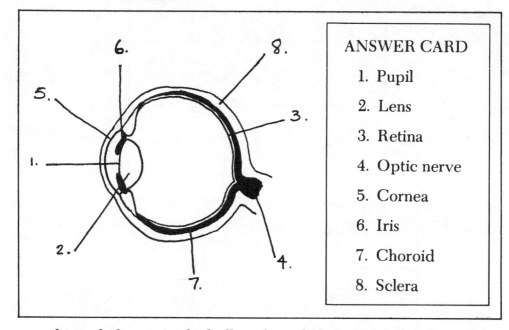

ANSWER CARD

1. Pupil
2. Lens
3. Retina
4. Optic nerve
5. Cornea
6. Iris
7. Choroid
8. Sclera

this and place it on the bulletin board. Compare your chart with the others.

Evaluation

You will evaluate your work by using the self-checking cards wherever possible, and through feedback from your classmates and teacher on your charts and models.

On Your Own

1. Look in your reference books to see how the eye and a camera are alike. Make a drawing or model to show the similarities. Place your work on the display table. Be prepared to explain it to the class.

2. In your reference books look up the history of eyeglasses. Why are some people nearsighted? farsighted? crosseyed? Find out how eyeglasses help them to see better. Write a report, using illustrations wherever possible. Post your report on the bulletin board.

3. Interview your school nurse to find out how a vision test is administered. Write up your interview.

4. Look in the reference books to find out why we see better with two eyes than with one. Try to find a simple experiment that will illustrate this. Be prepared to demonstrate and explain this to the class.

5. Do a poll of all the students at your grade level. Find out how many of them wear glasses, what is wrong with their eyes, how long they have worn glasses. Make a chart to present your information.

6. Interview someone who wears contact lenses, or an eye doctor, and find out the advantages and disadvantages of contact lenses over eyeglasses.

Suggestions for the Teacher—Learning Center No. 24

Objective

This center is essentially self-teaching. It is developed in a way that stimulates children to learn certain facts about the eyes on a totally independent basis. It frees the teacher to devote direct teaching time to more difficult or abstract concepts. It also promotes the pupils' independent research skills.

Suggestions for Making the Center

1. Use a sheet of colored posterboard or cardboard as the background. Draw a large, clear diagram of the eye on the background, or draw it on a separate sheet of paper and mount it to the background. You might do this by using an opaque projector to project an appropriate picture from a book onto the paper and tracing it. Or you can make a transparency of the

picture of the eye and project it with an overhead projector.

2. Scatter the names of the various parts of the eye on the posterboard.

3. Make a pocket for the Objectives, Materials, Directions, Evaluation and On Your Own activities.

4. Make four pockets for: Parts of Eye, Definitions and Uses, Quizzes, Answers.

5. Make up two sets of cards—one with the names of the various parts of the eye, and the other with the definitions and functions of each of these parts. Use a different color for each of the two sets for easy replacement in the pockets. Place matching numerals on the back of each pair of cards for self-checking. Place the cards in their pockets.

Suggested parts of the eye and their definitions and uses:

Eyelids	Outercoat, movable fold of skin that acts as cover.
Lachrymal glands	Produce tears to cleanse the eyes.
Sclera	The outer layer of the eyeball which serves as the supporting framework of the eye.
Cornea	The forward portion of the outer coat of the eyeball; allows light to enter the eye; shaped like an igloo.
Anterior chamber	Small space behind the cornea containing a watery fluid called aqueous humor which lubricates the eye.
Choroid	Membrane between sclera and retina; contains blood vessels that nourish the middle layer of the eye.
Ciliary muscle	A muscle that keeps the lens in place; part of the middle layer.

Lens	Receives the picture of what we see and transmits it to the retina.
Iris	A thin curtain of tissue over the lens; regulates the size of the pupil; determines the color of the eyes.
Pupil	A round hole in the iris through which light enters the eye.
Retina	A membrane that lines the eyeball and receives the picture from the lens, sending it through the optic nerve to the brain.
Optic nerve	The large nerve that carries the picture we see to the brain.

6. Make up and run off copies of the Crossword Puzzle and Eye Diagram. (Samples given.) Put them in the Quizzes pocket. Make up answer cards for each puzzle and put them in the Answers pocket.

7. Provide display space for the models of the eye and bulletin board space for drawings, reports and charts made by pupils.

Discussion

One of the strengths of this center is that it is set up to be used by pairs of children from beginning to end. It may take several weeks before all children complete it. Schedule time for presentations, demonstrations, discussion of completed work.

Remember that this is primarily a self-teaching center—let it work for you. Provide the materials, offer guidance by answering questions and making suggestions, and, most important, provide for sharing of products and information.

Make available at least one set of encyclopedias as well as a number of science books. Particularly recommended books are: *Read About the Eye* by Kathleen Elgin (New York, Franklin Watts, 1967) *The How and Why Wonder Book of the Human*

Body by Martin Keen (New York, Grosset and Dunlap, 1974) *The Human Body* by Mitchell Wilson (New York, Golden Press, 1968) and *Our Wonderful Eyes* by John Perry (New York, McGraw Hill, 1955).

BIBLIOGRAPHY

A Challenge for Change, Interning for Learning, Rio Grande, N.J.: Rio Grande Elementary School, 1973.

Berger, Evelyn and Bonnie Winters, *Social Studies in the Open Classroom*, Columbia University, N.Y.: Teacher's College Press, 1973.

Blitz, Barbara, *The Open Classroom: Making It Work*, Boston, Mass.: Allyn and Bacon, 1973.

Brown, Rosellen, et. al., *The Whole Word Catalogue*, N.Y.: Teachers and Writers Collaborative, 1972.

Buice, Audrey Ann and Mary Ann Heltshe, *Reading with a Smile (90 Reading Games that Work)*, Washington, D.C.: Acropolis Books Ltd., 1975.

Carswell, Evelyn M. and Darrell L. Roubinals, *Open Sesame: A Primer in Open Education*, Pacific Palisades, Calif.: Goodyear Publishing Co., Inc., 1974.

*Carter, Rachel, *Kit of Learning Center Activities*, Greenboro, N.C.: Carolina Education Center, 1973.

Cole, Ann, et. al., *I Saw a Purple Cow*, Boston: Little, Brown & Co., 1972.

*Cole, Ann, et. al., *Recipes for Fun*, Northfield, Ill.: Par Project, 1974.

*Collier, Mary Jo, Imogene Forte, and Joy McKenzie, *Kids' Stuff, Kindergarten and Nursery School*, Nashville, Tenn.: Incentive Publications, 1969.

*Collier, Mary Jo, Imogene Forte, and Joy McKenzie, *Kids' Stuff, Reading and Spelling, Primary Level*, Nashville, Tenn.: Incentive Publications, 1969.

Creative Moments: 50 Activity Folders for Fun and Challenge, Kits 1 and 2, Boston, Mass.: Creative Studies, Inc., 1972.

---

*Contain very practical ideas for centers.

Dale, Edgar, et. al., *Techniques of Teaching Vocabulary*, Chicago: Field Educational Publications, 1971.

*Davidson, Tom, et. al., *The Learning Center Book*, Pacific Palisades, Calif.: Goodyear Publishing Co., 1976.

Dean, Joan, *Recording Children's Progress*, Englewood Cliffs, N.J.: Citation Press, 1972.

Dean, Joan, *Room to Learn: Language Arts*, Englewood Cliffs, N.J.: Citation Press, 1973.

Devaney, Kathleen, *Developing Open Education in America*, Washington, D.C.: National Association for the Education of Young Children, 1974.

*Don, Sue, Jack W. Humphrey, et. al., *Individualizing Reading Instruction with Learning Stations and Centers*, Evansville, Ind.: Riverside Learning Associates, Inc., 1973.

Elementary English, (Entire issue devoted to open education), March 1973.

*Engel, Brenda A., *Arranging the Informal Classroom*, Newton, Mass.: Educational Development Center, 1973.

*Farnette, Cherrie, Imogene Forte and Barbara Loss, *Kids' Stuff, Reading and Writing Readiness*, Nashville, Tenn.: Incentive Publications, 1974.

*Farnette, Cherrie, Imogene Forte and Barbara Loss, *Special Kids' Stuff*, Nashville, Tenn.: Incentive Publications, 1976.

Featherstone, Joseph, *Schools Where Children Learn*, N.Y.: Liveright, 1971.

*Forte, Imogene, Marge Frank and Joy McKenzie, *Kids' Stuff, Intermediate - Jr. High*, Nashville, Tenn.: Incentive Publications, 1970.

*Forte, Imogene, Mary Ann Pangle and Robbie Tupa, *Cornering Creative Writing*, Nashville, Tenn.: Incentive Publications, 1974.

*Forte, Imogene and Joy McKenzie, *Nooks, Crannies, Corners*, Nashville, Tenn.: Incentive Publications, 1972.

*Forte, Imogene, Mary Ann Pangle, and Robbie Tupa, *Center Stuff for Nooks, Crannies, Corners*, Nashville, Tenn.: Incentive Publications, 1973.

*Forte, Imogene, Mary Ann Pangle and Robbie Tupa, *More Center Stuff for Nooks, Crannies and Corners*, Nashville, Tenn.: Incentive Publications, 1975.

*Garrison, Evangeline, *Individual Reading Self-Pace Activities*, Dansville, N.Y.: Instructor Publications, 1970.

Gerbrandt, Gary L., *An Idea Book for Acting Out and Writing Language*, Urbana, Ill.: National Council for Teachers of English, 1974.

Gilstrap, Robert L. and William R. Martin, *Current Strategies for Teachers*,

---

*Contain very practical ideas for centers.

Pacific Palisades, Calif.: Goodyear Publishing Co., Inc., 1975.

Glasser, Joyce F., *The Elementary School Learning Center for Independent Study*, West Nyack, N.Y.: Parker, 1971.

*Godfrey, Lorraine Hunt, *Individualizing with Learning Stations*, Menlo Park, Calif.: Individualized Books Publishing Co., 1974.

Greff, Kasper N., Mary College and Eunice Askov, *Learning Centers: An Idea Book for Reading and Language Arts*, Dubuque, Iowa: Kendall Hunt Publishing Co., 1974.

Handbook of Learning Centers (Books 1-4, grade levels K-6), Clarksville, Md.: Board of Education of Howard County, 1973.

Hearn, D.D., et. al., *Current Research and Perspectives in Open Education*, Washington, D.C.: American Association of Elementary, Kindergarten and Nursery Education (EKNE), undated.

*Herr, Selma E., *Learning Activities for Reading*, 2nd edition, Dubuque, Iowa: Wm. C. Brown, publishers, 1961, 1970.

Hertzberg, Alvin and Edward F. Stone, *Schools Are For Children*, N.Y.: Shocken Books, 1971.

Holt, John, *What Do I Do On Mondays?*, N.Y.: Dell Publishing Co., 1970.

Horton, Lowell and Phyllis Horton, *The Learning Center: Heart of the School*, Minneapolis, Minn.: T.S. Dennison and Co., 1973.

Hurwitz, Abraham B. and Arthur Goddard, *Games to Improve Your Child's English*, N.Y.: Simon & Schuster, 1970.

Instructo Corporation, Paoli, Pa., Publishes about 30 commercially-made centers for language arts and mathematics.

Kahl, David H. and Barbara J. Gest, *Learning Centers in the Open Classroom*, Encino, Calif.: International Center for Educational Development, 1974.

*Kaplan, Sandra Nina, JoAnn Kaplan, Sheila Madsen, and Bette Taylor, *Change for Children*, Pacific Palisades, Calif.: Goodyear Publishing Co., Inc., 1973.

*Kaplan, Sandra Nina, JoAnn Kaplan, Sheila Madsen, Bette Gould, *A Young Child Experiences*, Pacific Palisades, Calif.: Goodyear Publishing Co., Inc., 1975.

*Kaplan, Sandra Nina, Sheila Madsen, and Bette Gould, *The Big Book of Collections*, Pacific Palisades, Calif.: Goodyear Publishing Co., Inc., 1975.

*Kaplan, Sandra Nina, Sheila Madsen, and Bette Gould, *The Big Book of Writing*, Pacific Palisades, Calif.: Goodyear Publishing Co., Inc., 1975.

Kennedy, Leonard and Ruth Michen, *Games for Individualizing Math Learn-*

---

*Contain very practical ideas for centers.

ing, Columbus, Ohio: Charles E. Merrill, 1973.

*King, Joyce and Carol Katzman, *Imagine That*, Pacific Palisades, Calif.: Goodyear Publishing Co., Inc., 1976.

**Language Arts Sampler, New Ways in Communication*, Cambridge, Mass.: Ealing Corp., 1968.

**Learning Stations and Centers*, Interning for Learning, Rio Grande, N.J.: Rio Grande Elementary School, 1973.

*Lloyd, Dorothy M., *70 Activities for Classroom Learning Centers*, Dansville, N.Y.: Instructor Publications, 1974.

*Lorton, Mary Baratta, *Workjobs*, Reading, Mass.: Addison-Wesley, 1972.

Mallett, Jerry J., *Classroom Reading Games Activity Kit*, N.Y.: The Center for Applied Research in Education, Inc., 1975.

*Margrabe, Mary, *The Now Library: A Stations Approach Media Center Teaching Kit*, Washington, D.C.: Acropolis Books Ltd., 1973.

Marshall, Kim, *Opening Your Classroom with Learning Stations*, Palo Alto, Calif.: Learning Handbooks, 1975.

*Moore, Elaine and Jerri Greenlee, *Ideas for Learning Centers*, Belmont, Calif.: Leah Siegel/Fearon Publishers, 1974.

*Morlan, John, *Classroom Learning Centers*, Belmont, Calif.: Leah Siegel/Fearon Publishers, 1974.

*Mulac, Margaret E., *Educational Games for Fun*, N.Y.: Harper & Row, 1971.

Pearson, Craig and Joseph Marguffi, *Creating and Using Learning Games*, Palo Alto, Calif.: Learning Handbooks, 1975.

Pearson, Eric, *Trends in School Design*, Englewood Cliffs, N.J.: Citation Press, 1972.

Peck, Matilda J. and Morton A. Schultz, *Teaching Ideas That Make Learning Fun*, West Nyack, N.Y.: Parker Publishing Co., 1969.

*Perlman, Esther, *201 Learning Center Ideas*, Bryn Mawr, Pa.: I. Red Co., 617 Morris Ave., 1973.

Pidgeon, Douglas A., *Evaluation of Achievement*, Englewood Cliffs, N.J.: Citation Press, 1972.

*Pierrors, Betty, *How to Create Reading Centers*, Carson, Calif.: Educational Insights, Inc., 1974.

*Rapport, Virginia, *Learning Centers: Children on Their Own*, Washington, D.C.: Association for Childhood International, 1970.

Rathbone, Charles H., ed., *Open Education*, Englewood Cliffs, N.J.: Citation Press, 1972.

---

*Contain very practical ideas for centers.

Raths, Louis, et. al., *Teaching for Thinking*, Columbus, Ohio: Charles E. Merrill, 1967.

Schaaf, Joanne, *The Language Arts Idea Book*, Pacific Palisades, Calif.: Goodyear Publishing Co., Inc., 1976.

Silberman, Charles, *The Open Classroom Reader*, N.Y.: Vintage Books, 1973.

Silberman, Melvin L., et. al., *The Psychology of Open Teaching and Learning*, Boston, Mass.: Little, Brown, and Co., 1972.

Simini, Megan L., *Contemporary Language Activity Cards*, Englewood Cliffs, N.J.: Prentice-Hall, 1975.

*Stahl, Donna Kojak and Patricia Anzalone, *Individualized Teaching in Elementary School*, W. Nyack, N.Y.: Parker Publishing Co., 1970.

Story Starters, Sets 1 and 2, Monterey Park, Calif.: Creative Teaching Press, Inc., 1972.

Taylor, Joy, *Organizing the Open Classroom*, N.Y.: Schocken Books, 1972.

The Individualized Learning Letter (T.I.L.L.), 67 E. Shore Drive, Huntington, N.Y., 11743, 18 issues annually.

*Thomas, John I., *Learning Centers: Opening Up the Classroom*, Boston: Holbrook Press, Inc., 1975.

Thompson, Richard A., *Energizers for Reading Instruction*, West Nyack, N.Y.: Parker Publishing Co., 1973.

*Tiedt, Iris and Sidney Tiedt, *Elementary Teachers' Complete Idea Handbook*, Englewood Cliffs, N.J.: Prentice-Hall, 1965.

Vance, Frank, et. al., *Classroom Interest Centers*, Iowa City: Special Education Curriculum Development Center, University of Iowa, 1971.

*Voight, Ralph, *Center Teaching with Instructional Depth*, Wash., D.C.: Acropolis Books Ltd., 1974.

*Voight, Ralph, *Invitation to Learning: The Learning Center Handbook*, Wash., D.C.: Acropolis Books, Ltd., 1974.

*Volkmer, Clara B., et. al., *Structuring the Classroom for Success*, Columbus, Ohio: Charles E. Merrill, 1974.

Wagner, Guy, et. al., *Educational Games and Activities*, N.Y.: Macmillan, 1966.

Warman, Richard S., ed., *Yellow Pages of Learning Resources*, Cambridge, Mass.: M.I.T. Press, 1972.

*Waynant, Louise and Robert Wilson, *Learning Centers: A Guide for Effective Use*, Paoli, Pa.: Instructo Corp., 1974.

Your Green Pages, Darien, Conn.: Early Years Magazine, 1972.

---

*Contain very practical ideas for centers.

APPENDIX

CONTRACT FORM

Name _____

Write the numbers of the centers you intend to do each day.
Circle the numbers of the centers you complete.

DATE	CENTER NUMBERS						

Weekly Center or Free Choice Activities

Name _____ *Week of* _____

DAY	TIME	What are you going to do?	Where are you going to work?	What books and materials will you use?	What did you accomplish?

OFFICIAL CONTRACT

For this week of _____ , I, _____
                      (dates)   *(name)*
pledge to visit Learning Centers Numbers _____

I will also listen to these books _____

in the Listening Center.

If I am asked to visit more centers or read more, I will do so with a smile.

Signature _____

Witnessed by _____

Date _____

OFFICIAL CERTIFICATE

This certificate is awarded to _____

for fulfilling the contract and completing the work promised for

the week of _____ .

(☺) HOORAY!   _____
                                      Teacher's signature

CONTRACT FORM

*Week of*_____   *Name* _____

Check the left-hand side of the box for centers you plan to work at.
Check the right-hand side of the box for centers you complete.
Write *completed* across the line for centers you have completed in previous weeks.

Center No.	Monday	Tuesday	Wednesday	Thursday	Friday
1					
2					
3					
4					
5					
6					
7					
8					
9					

CONTRACT FORM

Name ——————————— *Week of* ———————————

This week I will work at the following three centers:

Number Name	When Completed

I will also spend time at the following reading activities:

	Title and/or Pages	When Completed
Basal Reader		
Library Book		
Film Strip Story		
Skill Practice		

MY PLANS

Name ——————————— *Week of* ———————————

In each block write some brief notes for what you plan to complete at each center.

Center	Monday	Tuesday	Wednesday	Thursday	Friday
Reading					
Math					
Writing					
Language Arts					
Social Studies					
Science					
Others					
My Day ☺ ☺ ☹					

Schedule and Evaluation Sheet*

NAME: _____   *Week of:* _____

	MONDAY	TUESDAY	WEDNESDAY	THURSDAY	FRIDAY
9:00 - 9:30	STATIONS	STATIONS	CHOICE	STATIONS	CHOICE
9:30 - 10:00	INSTR. READING	INSTR. READING	STATIONS	INSTR. READING	STATIONS
10:00 - 10:30	FOLLOW-UP	FOLLOW-UP	INSTR. READING	FOLLOW-UP	INSTR. READING
10:30 - 11:00	INSTR. SOCIAL STUDIES	INSTR. LANGUAGE	INSTR. LANGUAGE	INSTR. LITERATURE	INSTR. SOCIAL STUDIES

STATIONS COMPLETED

1	2	3	4	5	6	7	8
9	10	11	12	13	14	15	16
17	18	19	20	21	22	23	24
25							

CHOICE TIME	W	F
Writing		
Viewing		
Art		
Word Bank		
Comp. Station		
Library		
Puzzle		

STUDENT'S SELF EVALUATION

I made progress in _____

_____

I had trouble with _____

_____

TEACHER'S EVALUATION

Work Habits _____

Handwriting _____

Group Discussion _____

*Developed by Paul R. Daniels, Johns Hopkins University. Used by permission.

TALL TALES LEARNING CENTER*

PERSONAL RECORD OF_____

	Starting Date	Completion Date	Pupil Comment	Teacher Comment
Activity Starter				
Activity I				
Activity II				
Activity III				
Activity IV				
Activity V				
Activity VI				
Ditto Activity A				
Ditto Activity B				
Ditto Activity C				

A message from "The Boss": Please keep this sheet in your folder at all times. Thanks much!!

_____

*Used with permission from James B. MacCall and Marianne E. Straub.

Learning Center Record Sheet

Student's Name _____

Name and Number of Learning Center	Date Begun	Date Finished	Teacher's Remarks

WORK PLANNER FOR _____

(name)

WEEK OF_____

(dates)

Write the number of each center you plan to do each day.
Write also what you plan to do during any free time you
have.

☺ HAVE A GOOD DAY!

MONDAY   _____

_____

_____

TUESDAY   _____

_____

_____

WEDNESDAY _____

_____

_____

THURSDAY   _____

_____

_____

FRIDAY   _____

_____

_____

Name

Date

This Week Was:

SUPER

GOOD

OKAY

POOR

TERRIBLE

Color the thermometer.

Tell why you colored the thermometer as you did.

Primary Self-Evaluation Sheet*

Student's Name

Center Number	Date Completed	How I Think I Did
		☺ 😐 ☹
		☺ 😐 ☹
		☺ 😐 ☹
		☺ 😐 ☹
		☺ 😐 ☹
		☺ 😐 ☹
		☺ 😐 ☹

*Adapted from Interning for Learning, Title III, ESEA, Cape May County, New Jersey.

Individual Record Sheet

Student's Name	*Teacher's Name*

Centers Completed	Date	Evaluation
Projects Worked On		
Skill Builders Used:		
Reading: Math:		

A HANDBOOK FOR PARENTS*

Welcome to third grade! I'm looking forward to the pleasure of getting to know you and your child.

With the help of this booklet, I hope you will come to learn a little more about your child's teacher and the philosophy of our classroom.

*Prepared by Patricia Douglass, Edgewood Elementary School, Ridley School District, Folsom, Pa. Used by permission.

Our third grade curriculum affords your child the opportunity to review old skills, and to acquire new ones. Presented in summary form is the program we hope to follow during the school year.

READING   In third grade, children change teachers for their reading and spelling period. They are grouped by their present reading level. As they progress, they may be reassigned to another group and in some cases, to another teacher. Each child receives a word list to accompany the book he/she is using in class. Please go over these words with your child.

SPELLING   Spelling is taught by the reading teacher. Generally, each teacher gives a spelling test at the end of each week. Some teachers hold a trial test during the middle of the week. If a child receives an "A" on the trial test, he does not take the final test.

Communication between the reading teacher and the classroom teacher is good. If your child is having some type of problem, you will be notified by your child's reading teacher, or by me.

LANGUAGE   During our language periods we will cover such things as punctuation, capitalization, correct word usage, and we will be writing letters and creative stories. Your child will also have a chance to listen to and discuss stories, poems and records. The "Sharing Time" lets your child show and discuss something that interests him/her with the class, and provides practice in good speaking and listening skills.

HANDWRITING   At the beginning of the school year, printing is still used. During late October or early November the transition to cursive writing begins. For those children experiencing difficulty, extra practice is given.

SOCIAL SCIENCES Throughout the year, group discussions, films and simple research projects are used to help your child learn more about other people's lives as well as his own. Some of the topics we plan to study include learning about people and their behavior; map skills; Indian culture; and life in foreign countries.

SCIENCE   In science your child will have the opportunity to perform simple experiments using the skills of the scientist—observing, testing and recording results.

MATH   In math the children work two and three place addition and subtraction problems. Later in the year multiplication and very simple division are introduced. Some time is also spent on sets, money, and telling time.

A DAY IN SCHOOL

As with children, no two school days are exactly alike. There are, however, enough similarities between days to draw up a general schedule for you. On a visit to our room you might see these activities:

AM Activities	PM Activities
Reading	Handwriting
Math	Science
Language	Social Science
Diary Writing	Story Reading
	Center Work
	Sharing Time

In addition to daily classroom activities, your child has music, gym, art and library periods.

As you can see on the schedule, time is reserved for Center Work. Many parents have asked "What is a center? What does my child do at this time?"

A learning center is an independent activity which allows children to improve their work in a skill area, to discover new interests, and to express their creativity. Centers permit a child to be responsible for learning at his own level and speed. They also give the teacher time to work with small groups or individuals.

During center time children work alone or in small groups on their assigned or free choice activities. Many of the tasks at a center are self-checking. This allows children to see immediately how well they have done. The completed work papers from centers are placed in each child's folder. During the child's conference with me this work is discussed.

A note on homework—Very little "homework" is given. Sometimes children must complete work started in class at home. This should not take much longer than a half hour.

A note on discipline—Most "problems" can be handled during the school day. You will be notified about serious problems.

It is important that I keep you informed of your child's school progress. Some of the ways in which this is accomplished are:

(1) Children's own evaluation sheets—Your child grades his own weekly progress in math, language and handwriting. This evaluation sheet does not have to be returned. (Sample sheet attached)

(2) Work contract conference—After the work on the contract is completed, individual conferences are held to review classwork and center papers. This contract paper is to be signed by you, and returned. (Sample attached)

Date _____ NAME _____

How Did You Do This Week?

Put a mouth on the face to show how *you* think you did.

⌢ = Poor   — = Average   ⌣ = Good

	Monday	Tuesday	Wednesday	Thursday	Friday

MATH

😐 😐 😐 😐 😐

LANGUAGE

😐 😐 😐 😐 😐

HANDWRITING

😐 😐 😐 😐 😐

Date _____ NAME _____

WORK CONTRACT

This week I will do the following work in:

MATH: *(textbook, workbook or worksheet names, pages or numbers)*

LANGUAGE: *(specific assignment: letter, poem, composition, story or skill practice sheet)*

HANDWRITING: *(forms needing practice)*

OTHER THINGS: _____
_____
_____
_____

CENTERS: *(names and numbers)* _____

HOW I DID MY WORK	M	T	W	Th	F
1. I was busy and quiet.					
2. I did my own work.					
3. I followed directions.					
4. I finished my work.					
5. I was a good listener.					
6. I shared materials.					
7. I was careful of materials.					

I need help in _____

_____

_____

At my conference we talked about_____

_____

_____

_____   _____
(TEACHER'S SIGNATURE)   (PARENT'S SIGNATURE)